IN ASSOCIATION WITH

THE NATIONAL VIDEOGAME ARCADE

ä HISTORY OF VIDEOGAMES

in 14 consoles, 5 computers, 2 arcade cabinets
...and an Ocarina of Time

IN
ASSOCIATION
WITH

THE
NATIONAL
VIDEOGAME
ARCADE

THIS IS A CARLTON BOOK

First published in 2018 by Carlton Books Ltd
20 Mortimer Street
London W1T 3JW

10 9 8 7 6 5 4 3 2

A CIP catalogue record for this book is available from the British
Library.

Editorial: Roland Hall
Design: Russell Knowles
Production: Emily Noto

ISBN: 978 1 78739 064 5

Printed in Dubai

IN ASSOCIATION WITH

THE NATIONAL VIDEOGAME ARCADE

A HISTORY OF VIDEOGAMES

in 14 consoles, 5 computers, 2 arcade cabinets
...and an Ocarina of Time

Iain Simons & James Newman

Foreword by Ian Livingstone

CARLTON
BOOKS

CONTENTS

FOREWORD

Games seem to follow me around, and I certainly follow them around. I'm always on the lookout for exciting new games to play.

I've spent my entire working life immersed in different kinds of play. I was lucky enough to turn my hobby into a career. From founding Games Workshop in 1975, selling the first Dungeons & Dragons boxes to a curious public, to creating Fighting Fantasy gamebooks, to helping bring Lara Croft and Tomb Raider into the global consciousness, to backing the mega-hit mobile game Golf Clash, to now working with Sumo Digital on a new generation of videogames. Life has been a game.

Generally, whilst games are loved by the millions of people who play them, I've found that games have never quite received the respect they deserve from the media. You might assume that I'm talking about videogames, but even Fighting Fantasy gamebooks were treated with equal moral suspicion when in reality they got a whole

generation of children reading in the 1980s. The problem is the word 'game' seems to send people in some quarters into a frenzy. Despite all the love from players, the cultural impact, the tens of thousands of jobs created, and the billions of pounds in revenue generated from games – it's been a bumpy road.

I never dreamed when I started out in this industry that one day there would be a National Videogame Arcade in the UK, and I would be writing the introduction to a book about its remarkable collection. Times are certainly changing.

And what a collection it is. I'm not saying that just because it has a couple of things in it with my name on them, but because it is unique in how it illustrates how diverse videogame culture is. This is a book about videogames with barely any games in it!

Instead, the NVA is inviting you to discover games through art, toys, fan-drawn maps, costumes, marketing materials, controllers, pirated software, mints and yes – bottles of

'Larazade'. The story of games can be told in a lot of different ways, and this is definitely a very different one. I hope you'll recognize some of the objects in the book and enjoy discovering (or rediscovering) this story about games. Lots of people have a videogame story – this book invites you to think about your own.

In a world of digital downloads, it's easy to forget how tactile the world of videogames still is. The feel of a controller, the amazing constructions of cosplayers, the astonishing effort of fan-made crafting. And whilst the games industry keeps marching towards digital distribution, players keep reminding us that the world of games is still very physical, too.

This book is about the world of games that we can touch, but more than that, it's about how the world of games touches us.

I hope you enjoy it.

Ian Livingstone

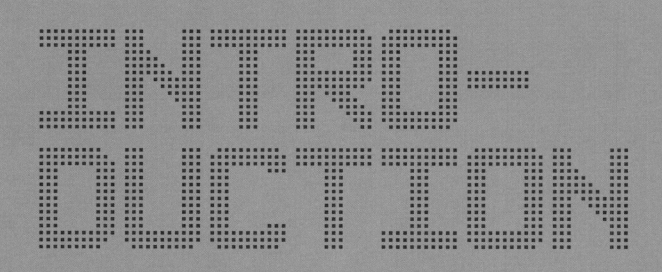

INTRO-
DUCTION

VIDEOGAMES
ARE THINGS

Ours is a digital age. It's an age of zeros and ones, data and code. And what could be more emblematic of this increasingly virtual world than the videogame? This is entertainment literally made of bits and bytes, pixels and sprites. Think about the way we describe the 'generations' of gaming. The '8-bit era' of pixelated graphics and chiptune bleeps and bloops gives way to the 16-bit era with higher resolution graphics, more colours, and richer sound, which, in turn leads to the 32-bit era of the PlayStation and so it continues... The most commonly told history of videogames is one in which increasingly powerful

processors capable of crunching more data more quickly and generating more impressive graphics and sound.

But that's only part of the story. Not only are those processors physical objects, they are encased in consoles and computers with distinctive designs. Grey, black, multicoloured; futuristic or reassuringly familiar, each makes its own statement. And each system has an interface with its own distinctive qualities. Each keyboard feels different, each mouse button makes a different clicking sound, each joystick fire button has a shape that makes it sit in a particular way under your thumb.

And, let's not forget that for decades all that data and code that gave rise to the spectacular graphics, sounds and game-play have been stored and distributed on cartridges, discs and cassettes. Pieces of plastic and metal. Physical objects. Things. And these things, too, have their own unique shape, look and feel. Some cartridges are huge, while others are almost impossibly tiny. Some are adorned with colourful labels, while others are altogether more understated. Some cartridges contain batteries to save your progress (until they run out), others include special chips to enhance a system's capabilities or to add new

sensors capable of reading light levels or a player's physical movement in the world.

Even today, in which the process of buying a new game from an online store might feel like a wholly digital affair (right down to the electronic payment) with not a cartridge or disc in sight, there are still keyboards and joysticks to waggle, dance mats to pound on and touchscreens to, well, touch. And all this is before we even get to thinking about collectible merchandise, toys, t-shirts...

And so, although it may well be true that ours is an age enriched and shaped by the possibilities of digital technology, it's essential to remember that from the earliest days of Pong to the augmented reality of Pokémon Go, videogames are most definitely things, too.

BUT WHICH THINGS?

As curators at the UK's National Videogame Arcade (and people who have been playing all their lives), the opportunity to write about videogames is something we relish. We think videogames are important, we think they're often misunderstood, and we think they're invariably underappreciated. We really want to share what we think is exciting and innovative about the ways games are made, the ways they are marketed and sold, the ways they're controlled and played, and the incredibly creative and imaginative ways that players make new and unexpected things with them. With this in mind, we didn't want to write a book that

simply charted the Top 100 most influential games of all time, or the bestselling, or the best (whatever that might mean). So we didn't.

We wanted to produce a book that took a different look at the legacy of videogames. In one sense, you could argue that this isn't really a book about videogames at all. Or rather, it isn't a book only concerned with graphics and sound which is, after all, how we often think about videogames. This isn't a book full of screenshots of achingly beautiful character art that tell the technological story of how we have travelled from the first blips of light through to the photorealistic virtual actors in just a few decades.

Instead – and in keeping with The National Videogame Arcade's mission

to interpret and reinterpret videogame history – this is a book that focusses on the things we play with, the things games are made of, and the things games are made with. But we want to change how we think about videogames. That's why this is a book about joysticks, cartridges, discs and cassettes. It's a book about consoles and computers, keyboards and mice, joysticks and lightguns. But it's also a book about development documents and the processes of game making. It's about the hand-drawn maps lovingly created, edited and adapted by designers as they honed their game ideas. It's about the systems and technologies used by developers to write and test their code, hunting down every last bug and glitch before release day. And it's

also a book about players and fans who collect games, who buy magazines about games, who type in cheatcodes to unlock new features, and who hunt down every last bug and glitch left in the game to find hidden areas, items and characters so that they can make stories, models and artwork based on their findings.

In building the collection at the National Videogame Arcade for the exhibition that accompanies this book, we have gathered some truly unique objects. We have never-before-seen design documents detailing the development of Goldeneye 007, one of the most well-loved games of all time. We have a Nintendo NES console signed by none other than Masayuki Uemura, the former head of Nintendo's fabled 'R&D2' unit, who

led the team that gave us this most important of videogame consoles. And let us not forget the similarly unique work of gaming fans who produce their own one-off artworks using media from pens and pencils to hamabeads and LEGO. Though the creators of these works may not attain the fame or recognition of international developers, their creations are no less important parts of a participatory global gaming culture.

Of course, the significance of the objects in our collection cannot be measured by their rarity alone and this book is not simply a romp through 100 of the most hard-to-find or unique objects in the National Videogame Arcade's catalogue. Our history of gaming is one that recognizes the

importance of the ordinary, everyday objects whose very ordinary everydayness makes them easy to overlook.

And so, alongside our one-offs are mass-produced items so apparently plentiful that we could easily forget to capture and preserve them let alone consider their role in story of gaming. Objects like our Pokémon gashapon toy are eminently disposable and surely not designed to be kept forever, less still placed in a museum collection. Yet it is precisely their ephemeral nature that makes them so enduringly important.

After all, when they were creating them in the 1970s and 80s, did anybody really expect videogames to be the stuff of global cultural heritage or the subject of national museums'

collecting and curating work? Just because things seem to exist today in bountiful supply doesn't mean that they will always be with us. And as they are not always made to last, we have to actively sample, document and preserve them.

THE PEOPLE'S THINGS

Although this is a book about things, it is also ultimately a book about people. It's about the people that make games, play them and love them. It's about the objects they make them with, the objects they play with, and the objects of their affection, passion, labour and sometimes frustration. In

celebrating these objects, our mission is not to fill this book's pages with lingering photographs of mint-in-the-box items. In researching the book and building the National collection and accompanying exhibition, we didn't set out to source unopened examples of consoles or games that we can crack open in the photographic studio (you wouldn't be able to appreciate that 'new joypad' smell through a book anyway).

Although we're interested in things, we don't just want any things. We want things that players and developers have used. As such, rather than literally wipe away the traces of the people that made, owned and used our collection of videogame things,

we have chosen to leave them intact. In fact, we have chosen to celebrate them. This book already has fingerprints all over it, and just by picking it up, you're leaving yours on it now. You're adding to its history.

This isn't just a metaphor about detecting the hand of the developer through their design work or the presence of the player through the controller. We mean this literally. Within seconds of peeling back the protective wrapper on a tablet or smartphone that touchscreen is covered in greasy marks. It can't be helped. It's a touchscreen and that is what happens when you touch a screen. The same goes for a controller, a cartridge, or a CD... So if you're

wondering why we haven't cleaned off the fingerprints from the joysticks, why we haven't fixed the broken door on the front of the CRT or re-stuck the Sonic 2 stickers to the side panel, or why we haven't dusted the connectors on the computers and consoles, it precisely because these fingerprints, the peeling stickers, the detritus of pet hair and ground-in morsels of food are the evidence that these objects have a story to tell and that they have been used. Whether they were loved and cherished, whether they never lived up to expectations, or whether they were discarded, forgotten and then rediscovered, they were all designed, created and used by people.

PLAYTHINGS

This, then, is a book about videogames, but it is also a book about rethinking what videogames are. For sure, videogames are about graphics and sound, they are made of zeros and ones, data and code, bits and bytes and pixels and sprites, but they're so much more than that, too. They're physical and material. They are things we play with. They are playthings. But most importantly, let's not forget that they are things (and they're covered in fingerprints).

James Newman
and Iain Simons

001

30th Anniversary Mario amiibo

2015

The amiibo are Nintendo's entry into the 'toys to life' market. Having similar functionality to Activision's Skylanders, Disney Infinity and the LEGO Dimensions figures, amiibo figures can be tapped onto the Near Field Communication (NFC) reader built into the Nintendo Switch, Wii U or 3DS devices to enable new gameplay features or store player data in compatible software.

There is more to the resemblance to Skylanders than just a desire to capitalise on the series' success. Nintendo had originally been approached as a potential partner in the Skylanders project. They passed on the deal (although things have subsequently come full circle with characters from the Super Mario series now available as Skylanders figures).

This 8-Bit Super Mario amiibo was released in 2015 to coincide with the 30th anniversary of the original Japanese and US release of Super Mario Bros. for the Famicom/ Nintendo Entertainment System – the game was released in 1987 in Europe, but it was certainly nice to celebrate the 28th anniversary in the UK! It came as part of the Super Mario Maker special edition, along with a lavishly illustrated hardback art book crammed with hand-drawn level and character designs.

In one sense, the amiibo does a similar job to the art book in being a celebration of all things Mario. Tapped on the Wii U game pad, it transforms the Mario sprite into an oversized character (incidentally adding trademark moustaches to every item in the game) and changes the ordinarily pin sharp graphics to a simulation of a 1980s CRT TV set – all scan lines, blurriness and washed out colours.

But, there's more to this amiibo than a nostalgic recreation of the 80s. This is 8-Bit Mario, but it's 8-Bit Mario in 3D. This is no Mario that has ever existed in any game. Pixelated just like the 1985 plumber, but reimagined with more depth – literally. This extra dimension to the amiibo reminds us that Nintendo and Mario have always been at the forefront of gaming and game-play. 2D Mario elevated home gaming to new heights with its exquisite platforming action. Just over a decade later, Super Mario 64 revolutionised platform games by moving from 2D or 3D. You can almost chart the evolution of platform gaming by looking through the history of Super Mario releases.

The 8-Bit Mario amiibo is simultaneously 2D and 3D, retro and current, and all underpinned by the

+INFO

VARIATIONS: 2
CLASSIC COLOURS: RED OVERALLS WITH FLESH-COLOURED BUTTONS, BROWN BOOTS, SHIRT AND HAIR
MODERN COLOURS: BLUE OVERALLS WITH GOLD BUTTONS, RED SHIRT, DARK HAIR AND BOOTS
RELEASED: 11 SEPTEMBER 2015 (CLASSIC COLOURS), 23 OCTOBER 2015 (MODERN COLOURS)
NATIONAL MARIO DAY: 10 MARCH – MAR10

cutting edge new technology of Near Field Communication. It's Nintendo saying that Mario doesn't only represent the company's present and future but that Nintendo is the past, present and future of gaming. Oh, and like the other amiibo, it's also a really cool collectible figure that you can sit on your bookshelf.

Fun fact, there are actually two versions of the 8-Bit Mario amiibo. The 'modern colours' version bedecks Mario in his more familiar blue overalls. This one puts the plumber in his 'original' brown overalls.

▶ Right: 8-Bit Mario Amiibo (original colours).

SUPER MARIO BROS. ♛ 30TH

002.

Age of Empires III
Collectors' Edition

2005

ITEMS IN PACKAGE: 8
POSTER DIMENSIONS: 43 X 27 INCHES
POSTER CREATED BY: CRAIG MULLINS
MIGHTY CIVILISATIONS: 8
RECOMMENDED PROCESSOR SPEED: 1.4GHZ
NUMBER OF TRACKS ON SOUNDTRACK CD: 27
NUMBER OF PAGES IN THE ART OF EMPIRES BOOK: 208

Age of Empires, a real-time strategy game first released in 1997, has sold over 20 million copies to date, and spans several centuries in its historic scope. Age of Empires III, released in 2005, focussed on the European colonization of the Americas. The collectors' edition of AoE III is just contained by its box. It's a big game. It deserves a big box.

That said, ironically the game itself occupies very little space within this weighty block of heft. The slight CD-ROM containing the software is nestled at the bottom, encased by a cornucopia of materials telling the story of how it was created. This isn't any copy of Age of Empires III, this is the collectors' edition. A definitive celebration of not just the finished game, but how it came into existence.

The package is weighty. It would hurt you if it fell on you. The board game-like box is so tightly packed that it takes some effort to reassemble again, should you ever want to close the lid. Information about the game bursts out, a celebration of the process of its creation.

Anything you might require is included: a making of behind-the-scenes DVD; a full colour poster; the manual for the game; a players guide; and a soundtrack audio CD. Dominating the package though, is a

hardback 210-page book documenting the art from the series. This is no book of lavish final renders, though. The book is at pains to share the process, the sketches, the drafts, the effort that the creators have gone through to deliver the final game. Flicking through it summons up the spirit of engineering notebooks, DaVinci-esque sketches, roughing out concepts to compare with the final artwork alongside. Fittingly, as in an art catalogue, illustrations within it are attributed to individual artists. Even the smallest character renders bear the name of their creators. In a game of this scale, it's becomes a testament to their toil. The pomp with which the package has been produced underlines

it, but it's hard not be awed by the scale of the production.

At the bottom of it all, in a cardboard sleeve, sits a second distillation of those thousands of hours of effort. Another CD-ROM, a stripped-down demonstration version of the game. A gift for you to pass on, although one imagines that most collectors would want to keep this collectors' edition complete.

▲ Above: Age of Empires III Collectors' edition, all items.

◀ Right (above): Age of Empires III Collectors' Edition retail packaging.

▶ Right: Details from art books.

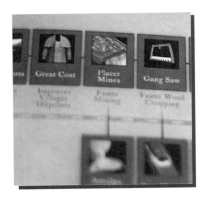

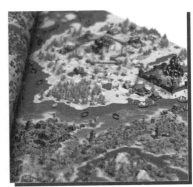

003.

Aladdin
Deck Enhancer

1992

+INFO

INVENTED BY: RICHARD DARLING
ADDITIONAL MEMORY: 64K
DIZZY THE ADVENTURER COMPACT CARTRIDGE: INCLUDED
ACCORDING TO THE PACKAGING, "ALADDIN IS THE FUTURE IN CONSOLE GAME PLAY"
COMPATIBLE GAMES: 7
COMPACT CARTRIDGE GAMES ANNOUNCED BUT NOT RELEASED INCLUDE BIG NOSE THE CAVEMAN, CJ'S ELEPHANT ANTICS AND GO! DIZZY GO!

To understand the Aladdin Deck Enhancer, you really need to dig back into the history of the videogames industry. That word 'dig' is an unfortunate but, sadly, appropriate one when we remember the impact of the slew of low-quality software and collapse in consumer and retailer confidence that led to Atari burying hundreds of thousands of cartridges in a landfill site.

On exporting its Famicom system, renamed the Nintendo Entertainment System, Nintendo sought to remedy some of what it saw as Atari's failings by placing far stricter controls on who could produce games for its system. It did this partly through its 'Seal of Quality' scheme and partly by building a technical lock into the console. This 10NES chip, as it was called, could only be unlocked when an authorized cartridge was inserted. Guess who controlled who was given the key? Nintendo got to restrict who developed for its system, and to collect revenue from them at the same time. Win-win. For Nintendo anyway.

Because it was expensive to develop for the NES, and there were limits on the number of games any publisher could produce in a year, people soon started looking for workarounds. One was to create subsidiary companies, and use these subsidiaries' yearly release

allocations to publish more games, which is what Acclaim did with its LJN division. Another option was to try to pick the 10NES' digital lock – which is where the Aladdin Deck Enhancer comes in.

Created by Richard Darling of UK developers Codemasters, and distributed by Camerica, the Aladdin Deck Enhancer is an adapter that contains circuitry capable of bypassing Nintendo's security checks. This allowed unlicensed games to be run on the NES. The unlicensed cartridge was slotted into the Aladdin adapter and played like any other. The Deck Enhancer also includes a memory controller and a graphics chip which, like the security bypass circuit, was intended to make the production of cartridges cheaper, as these resources didn't need to be added to each new product.

The Deck Enhancer was released in

November 1992, and it was announced that 24 games would be available for it by the end of 1993. Coming late in the NES' life cycle and with the SNES already hitting shelves, ultimately only seven compatible games were released for the Deck Enhancer – all, surprise surprise, from Codemasters and Camerica themselves. These included Micro Machines, Dizzy the Adventurer and Quattro Sports. Compatible cartridges can be immediately recognized by their physically smaller size – even the amount of plastic needed to make the cartridge was reduced, to drive down the cost of manufacture further.

▲ Above: Aladdin compatible Compact Cartridge retail packaging.

▶ Right: Aladdin Deck enhancer packaging (front and rear).

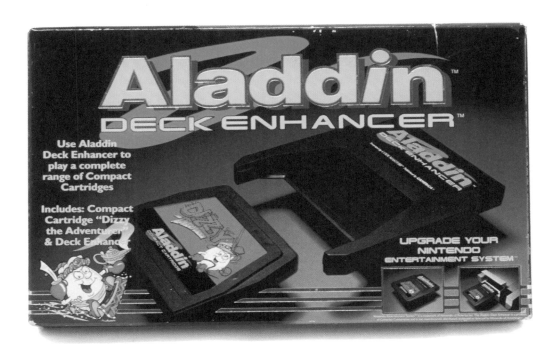

004

Apple Bandai Pippin

#INFO

DEVELOPER: APPLE
MANUFACTURER: BANDAI
AVAILABILITY: 1996–1997
PROCESSOR: POWERPC 603 RUNNING AT 66MHZ
UNITS SOLD: 42,000

The incredible success of the iPhone and iPad and the extraordinary number of games available in the iOS App Store have ensured that Apple are a key player in modern videogaming. This comes even though both the phone and tablet appear to lack the fundamental ingredients we've become used to in a gaming platform – namely the absence of physical buttons, joysticks, analogue or digital pads or any of the standard interface paraphernalia honed over decades. Nonetheless, and however unlikely a large rectangular slab of glass might seem as a gaming device, Apple is most definitely one of the key players in contemporary videogames. The 2017 revamp of the App Store separates out Games from all other Apps because games are just so important a part of what the phone and tablet are. They might as well just label the App Store as 'Games' and 'Everything Else'.

The prominence of games in the App Store or in keynote presentations that put demos of VR and AR centrestage is pretty surprising, when we remind ourselves that these are phones and tablets rather than dedicated gaming consoles. But it's even more surprising for anybody who has followed the history of computing over the past thirty or more years because the accepted wisdom for a long time was that Apple was never really interested in games.

Of course, there was the Apple II computer, which had plenty of games developed for it though it wasn't a games machine as such. Then in 1984 came the Macintosh, but that was always branded more as the computer for creatives doing desktop publishing, digital audio or video editing. Sure, there were games for the Mac, but game developers will tell you that Apple never really made it easy for them by providing programming tools or software libraries. And so this idea that Apple wasn't really concerned with games passed into folklore. But what this conveniently – or perhaps that should be 'deliberately' – forgets is the Pippin.

Named after a variety of Apple (just like the Macintosh) and released in Japan and the US in 1996, the Apple Bandai Pippin was a multimedia system and home videogame console. And that's the fact that even the most hardcore gamers might never have seen one let alone played on one probably gives you a sense of how successful it was.

Based on the Macintosh hardware and software and with a CD-ROM drive and dialup Internet connectivity, the Pippin could be connected to an ordinary TV set rather than a computer monitor and was designed for multimedia and gaming in the living room. One of the most striking features of the Pippin is its controller. Shaped like a boomerang and with a built-in trackball, it was named the Applejack (which is also the name of an Apple-based drink as well as a My Little Pony).

The system was a commercial failure with very few consoles sold. Among the many reasons for the failure were the high price of the system, the lack of software available and the almost non-existent marketing. These would be serious enough failures at the best of times. However, the Pippin was launching into a market in which Windows PCs, the Sega Saturn and Sony PlayStation were dominant. Even established players well experienced in the videogame industry like NIntendo would struggle against this competition. No matter how good software like Mr. Potato Head Saves Veggie Valley was, it was always going to struggle against wipEout and Ridge Racer. There was no hope for the Pippin. It may not have been rotten to the core but it was certainly one bad apple.

▶ Right: Apple Bandai Pippin unit and controller.

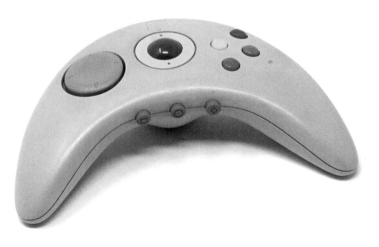

005.

Astro Wars

1981

✦INFO

DISPLAY TYPE: VFD (VACUUM FLUORESCENT DISPLAY)
POWER: 4 X C TYPE BATTERIES (6 VOLTS)
DIFFICULTY LEVELS: 4
1: ALIENS ATTACK SINGULARLY
2: AS DIFFICULTY 1 WITH INCREASED SPEED
3: ALIENS ATTACK IN PAIRS
4: AS DIFFICULTY 3 WITH INCREASED SPEED
MAXIMUM SCORE: 9999

In 1981, the world of video-gaming was still in the thrall of invading aliens and wars in space. Numerous titles had built on the basic model set out by Taito's original Space Invaders, adding new features such as aliens swooping down in waves to attack the player, as well as new eye and ear candy such as true multicolour graphics and musical jingles. It wasn't all additions, of course. Games like Namco's Galaxian removed Space Invaders' large 'bases' that provided some temporary shelter from the onslaught of enemy bullets. Now the player was exposed and alone in the endless vacuum of deep space.

Consoles such as the Atari 2600 brought some of the fun into the home, but they were expensive propositions, especially when you factored in the need for a television to play them on (and in an age where multi-set ownership was a vision of the future, this also meant delicate negotiations between *Dallas*, the news, an improving documentary about Renaissance art, and videogaming).

Enter the tabletop electronic gaming device. Not quite a console, not quite a handheld, but noisy and exciting nonetheless. Grandstand's Astro Wars, released in 1981, was one of the most popular of this category of gaming device. Licensed from Epoch

who would go onto create the dazzlingly mundane Barcode Battler, this was originally branded as Super Galaxian in Japan. Elsewhere, though, it was Astro Wars, which sounds altogether more Buck Rogers. And it was war. At the very least it was a war on the senses of the player.

The first thing that hits you is the sound. It's loud. It's not obnoxious, but it definitely has a brutal, electronic charm. The opening jingle that accompanies the beginning of the game is jolly enough but once it's played for the 100th time even the most hardcore Berlin techno fan would likely find it a little grating, as it distorts through the built-in speaker. The remainder of the sounds oscillate between a strange ticking effect as the aliens move and other assorted jingles which are very much variations on the original theme set out at the beginning.

The graphics have a similarly 80s feel to them. The display is small in part because of the Vacuum Fluorescent Display technology employed, although it is slightly magnified to make things more usable. If you've seen a Game & Watch, the segmented display will be familiar with every possible character ready to be illuminated rather than smoothly animated, as with modern graphics

systems, but you've not seen colours like these. Vivid and deep, in fact almost piercing, they are the perfect visual accompaniment for the shrill electronic sounds emanating from the unit.

The game-play itself takes the core of Galaxian and strips it down to its essentials (which is a novel definition of 'Super' and perhaps explains why the name was changed). Aliens attack, firing missiles as they drift down the screen. By flicking the reassuringly sturdy joystick, the player can steer their craft around in the hope that the bullets they loose off might hit home. Deal with enough waves of enemies and a landing sequence is initiated in which the ship splits in two and the top has to be docked with the bottom before the action starts again.

Different difficulty levels dictate the number and speed of the incoming enemies while leaving the core game-play unaltered. Even on the easiest level, game over often comes quickly, as the twitchy aliens and missiles rob the player of their five ships. However, unusually for a game of this period there is a definitive winning state, though the player has to be particularly skilled to see – or rather hear – it. Reach 9999 points, and a special jingle is played. Now there's an incentive to practise.

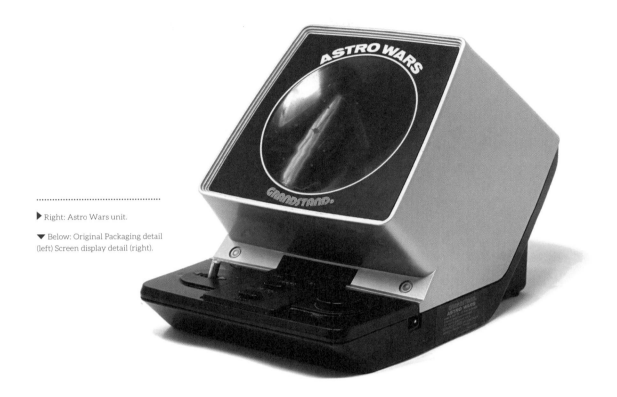

▶ Right: Astro Wars unit.

▼ Below: Original Packaging detail (left) Screen display detail (right).

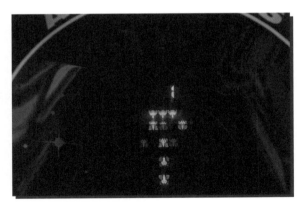

Atari 2600
1977

#INFO

PROJECT CODENAME: STELLA
BESTSELLING GAME: PAC-MAN
PART NUMBER: CX2600
PROCESSORS: MOS TECHNOLOGY 6507 RUNNING AT 1.19 MHZ (CPU), TIA (TELEVISION INTERFACE ADAPTER) FOR SOUND AND VIDEO
CASE VARIATIONS NICKNAMES: 'HEAVY SIXER', 'LIGHT SIXER' (BOTH WITH SIX SWITCHES ON THE FRONT), 'DARTH VADER' (ALL BLACK VERSION), '2600 JR' (SMALLER, REDUCED COST VERSION)
NUMBER OF BUTTONS ON JOYSTICK: ONE

Today, we are well used to talking about videogame 'platforms', but how often do we really stop to think about what this means, or whether there was a time when there were videogames but not platforms? Well, the answer to that last question is definitely 'yes'.

In the earliest days of home video-gaming, systems were hard coded to a single game. There were typically no general purpose microprocessors inside these systems, which instead were designed around bespoke hardware created specifically for the game in mind. Atari knew this model well having, manufactured Pong machines for the home that capitalized on the popularity and success of its tennis simulation in the arcades. But this was an expensive way of doing business and of designing games. By its very nature, dedicated hardware had to be designed each time a new game was created, and keeping up with fashions and trends was all the harder when you had to effectively reinvent the wheel each time.

Fortunately, developments in computing throughout the 1970s had suggested a way around the problem that didn't involve cassettes, floppy disks or other fragile media. A general purpose system with its own central processing unit (CPU), graphics and sound hardware and an interface slot that could accept cartridges that contained Read Only Memory (ROM) chips with new data for new games. What we had here was a platform. A single system that could be effectively reprogrammed every time a cartridge was inserted.

Developers would have a known specification to develop for and the whole business model would shift from selling one-off game systems to producing comparatively inexpensive consoles and generating continued sales and revenue with an ever-growing library of cartridges.

In fact, it wasn't Atari that brought the model to the videogame market first – The Magnavox Odyssey used additional curcuitboards for new games – Fairchild Semiconductor's 'Channel F' had offered removable ROM cartridges in 1976. However in 1977, Atari took what had been codenamed 'Stella' (named after one of the engineer's bicycles – true story!) and released it as the Video Computer System. The VCS (as it was abbreviated) would later go on to be renamed the Atari 2600 (after Atari's internal part reference number for the system) and was given a number of different cases from classic 1970s wood grain effects to sleeker 1980s plastic lines. But in whatever guise, the system would go on to dominate home video-gaming throughout the late 1970s and early 80s.

Nine games accompanied the system's launch, including Street Racer and Star Ship, but it was really the titles that came later that would define the 2600. Breakout, Space Invaders and Pitfall are three among many, many more. Pitfall is notable because it was created by Activision – a 'third party' (i.e. not Atari) developer. Again, the power of the platform ushered in an era of software companies established to develop games for other manufacturers' hardware platforms. If that sounds familiar to the videogame marketplace today, that's because it is.

▶ Right (top): Atari 2600 unit with joystick.

▶ Right (bottom) : Detail of 'Captain Atari' from the Atari Owner's Club application form.

BEAM ABOARD THE ATARI CLUB

Hi there Atari Owner

I'm Captain Atari, and it's my pleasure to welcome you to the space age world of computer video games.

Barbie® Careers
Game Developer Doll

2016

#INFO

STOCK KEEPING UNIT NUMBER: DMC33
SUITABLE FOR: AGES 3 AND UP
SERIES: 'CAREER DOLLS'
ACCESSORIES: TABLET, LAPTOP,
HEADSET MIC
RETAIL PRICE: $12.99

Originally launched in 1959 by US toy company Mattel, Barbie has had a number of jobs over the years including architect, NASCAR driver, vet and mermaid. In recent years, Mattel's 'Career Doll' series has focused on a 'career of the year' and in 2016 Barbie became a game developer.

According to Mattel, the aim of Game Developer Barbie is to inspire people into STEM education (Science Technology Engineering and Maths) through making games and learning to code. In Mattel's own words, you can:

'Explore the world of game development with the Barbie® game developer doll! Honored as a career of the year, young techies can play out the creative fun of this exciting profession. Barbie® doll looks casually cool in an industry-inspired outfit. Her t-shirt breaks the fashion code with a hip graphic; faded denim pants are tech trendy; a green jacket is fashion-forward with sleeves rolled up; and white sneakers. Vibrant red hair and bright matching glasses complete the authentic look. A laptop (with real game code graphics), tablet (with the game she is working on) and silvery headset expand the storytelling possibilities and career opportunities. Inspire young gamers with this doll who is at the top of her game!'

It's too early to tell how many people Game Developer Barbie has inspired to start making their own games, but it's almost certain that Mattel remembers its earlier attempt to enter the world of coding. Released in 2014, Computer Engineer Barbie caused controversy with some praising the choice of career and others pointing to the stereotyped clothing and accessories. The big problem, however, was the accompanying book. Titled, *I Can Be A Computer Engineer*, it painted a picture of Computer Engineer Barbie depending on the support of her two male coding friends to solve programming problems and accidentally infecting her and her sister's laptop with a virus by using a heart-shaped pink flash drive necklace against the clear advice of her teacher. Homework lost? Check. Music library lost? Check. Data recovered by male colleagues? Check.

Following widespread criticism of the book's content, Mattel withdrew the volume and apologized for its outdated content. Certainly Game Developer Barbie's laptop and tablet combo marks a step forward from Computer Engineer Barbie. According to academic Casey Fiesler, who studied the code printed on the tiny laptop screen:

'The interface appears to be Alice, an educational programming environment, and the code it's outputting is ActionScript (or maybe Haxe). Basically, she seems to be making a Bejeweled clone in Flash.'

It might not be the most groundbreaking piece of development, but it certainly beats the unrealistic and impenetrable array of 0s and 1s printed on Computer Engineer Barbie's laptop screen.

▲ Above: Detail of tablet computer accessory.

▶ Right: Barbie Careers Game Developer in original packaging.

Barcode Battler

1991

◆INFO

MANUFACTURER: EPOCH LTD
RELEASED: 1991 (BARCODE BATTLER II: 1992)
NEW BARCODE BATTLER II CARDS:
WIZARDS, MAGIC, SURVIVAL, NEWS
GAME MODES: 3 (C0 TWO PLAYER,
C1 AND C2 SINGLE PLAYER)
MAGIC POINTS AT GAME START: 10
LIGHT WORLDS PER ERA: 5

You might well ask yourself why the Barcode Battler didn't go on to change the face of popular entertainment. After all, everybody loves barcodes, right? Oh really? We thought everybody did. Maybe it's just us.

Well, us and the good people at Epoch, who came up with the idea for the Barcode Battler. Picture the scene. It's 1991. Street Fighter II has just been released in the arcades, and Sonic the Hedgehog has been unleashed on the Mega Drive. Exciting times, indeed. It's going to be difficult to really shake up the marketplace and innovate. This is going to need some lateral thinking. And you don't get much more lateral than barcodes (you like bad geometry puns as well, right?)

The idea behind the Barcode Battler is a simple one. Players use the handheld device to scan special cards whose printed barcodes represent different characters, enemies or power ups. Of course, the real excitement came when you realized that you weren't restricted to the supplied barcode cards. Suddenly, the kitchen cupboard was a treasure trove. That loaf of bread could be a powerful ally. Lurking in that tin of tuna for the cat could be an inimitable wizard.

Don't believe us that barcodes can be this exciting? Just listen to the UK TV advert... "They are all around us. Millions of barcode warriors and wizards waiting to fight. Waiting for Barcode Battler to free their awesome power".

Still not convinced? No, not many people were – not outside Japan anyway, where the Barcode Battler was actually pretty successful. So much so, in fact, that Epoch and Nintendo teamed up to create special edition cards with characters from the Super Mario and Legend of Zelda series. They even collaborated to develop the BBII Interface that allowed the Barcode Battler II (yes, there was a sequel) to connect to the Famicom and Super Famicom in order to play compatible games such as Barcode World and J-League '94.

In many ways, the Barcode Battler was ahead of its time and, years later, Nintendo revived the idea with its e-reader adapter for the Game Boy and its range of amiibo cards that add functionality to 3DS, Wii U and Switch games. But there's still nothing quite like the thrill of scanning the barcode and unlocking the powerful weapon from a bottle of toilet cleaner.

▲ Above: Barcode Battler packaging.

▶ Right: Barcode Battler.

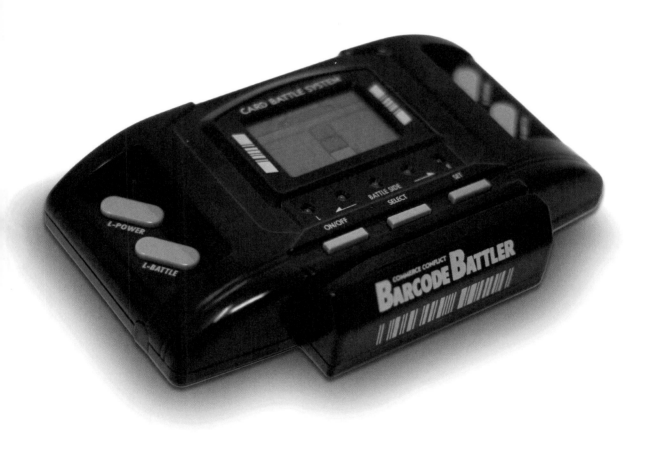

BASICODE 2
cassette
1984

It's now increasingly commonplace for our light bulbs to be connected to the internet, waiting to be activated by speech commands that have to be interpreted by a vast, cloud network of computational power, all to the end of lighting up our kitchen.

When computers first entered our homes in the 1980s, the impact was so disruptive, so revolutionary, that they even demanded a prefix. It was as if we needed reassurance that they were really, truly supposed to be there. HOME computers were computers that lived amongst us, with our loved ones. They shared in our day to day lives.

When they were unwrapped from their boxes, however, they didn't do much. They needed instructions, which were provided by computer code that their owner needed to input. Many of them shipped with a version of a language called BASIC (Beginners All-purpose Symbolic Instruction Code) for that purpose. BASIC was there to provide an easy way for the new computer owner to issue their instructions. But, as ever, this wasn't without problems.

Different hardware manufacturers inevitably produced different versions of BASIC for their machines.

Whilst they were similar in structure, the dialects were often radically different. Simple actions would require completely different commands on different machines, making it impossible to create a single computer program that would run on multiple machines. Today of course, that's expected, but in the early days of computing it was seen as something worth fighting against.

One answer to this problem emerged from a Dutch radio station, NOS, and was adopted and developed by a number of other public broadcasters, including the BBC.

BASICODE was conceived as being an 'Esperanto for computers'. It created a number of different interpreters for different host machines, allowing them to load and run the *same* 'BASICODE' programs. Thus, a Commodore 64 could run the same code as a ZX Spectrum. Perhaps the most radical stroke was in the distribution. The Radio stations themselves broadcast BASICODE software, inviting listeners to record it directly from transmission onto cassette tapes and load it into their computers.

There's probably no more powerful indicator of the domestication of

computers than this. Major public broadcasters took time in their schedules to transmit the beeps and whirrs of code for long periods of time. BBC Radio 4 (no less) invited listeners at home to press record and 'download' new BASICODE software to load into their interpreters. In doing so, of course, they also neatly demonstrated how easy it was to reproduce software using domestic tape recorders.

BASICODE was of course awkward, made huge demands on the user, and was destined to obsolescence as technology rapidly evolved. But as a marker of the hobbyist home computer movement and its dedication to open interoperability, it was a remarkable, beautiful effort.

+INFO

FIRST BROADCAST: DURING THE HOBBY-SCOOP PROGRAMME ON DUTCH RADIO BROADCASTER NOS (NEDERLANDSE OMROEP STICHTING)
AUDIO: MONOAURAL
COPYRIGHT: RADIO NETHERLANDS
DESIGN: BBC INFORMATION DIVISION
PROGRAMME 16: CAR RACE

▶ Right: BASICODE 2 cassette and retail packaging.

BBC Model B microcomputer

1981

#INFO

NICKNAME: 'THE BEEB'
RELEASED: 1 DECEMBER 1981
ORIGINAL PRICE: £335 (MODEL B)
NUMBER OF FUNCTION KEYS: 10; COLOUR OF
FUNCTION KEYS: RED/ORANGE; RAM: 32KB; VOICE
OF THE OPTIONAL SPEECH SYNTHESIS PACK-
AGE: KENNETH KENDALL (BBC NEWSREADER)

In recent years there's been a chorus of discontent from the global tech industry about the inadequate training that young people are receiving in computer science. They might know how to write a letter in a word processor, but they don't know how to write a word processor. Not enough people know how to code.

We're spoilt. You might have experienced how irritating it is to unbox a new computer, plug it in and have to wait a short while for it to download the updates to its operating system. Try and conceive of a time when computers were dumb things that didn't do ANYTHING unless you instructed them to, but I promise you it happened.

The early eighties in the UK was a remarkable period in the birth of videogames. A seismic innovation, made commercially viable by Sinclair and Commodore, which invaded living rooms and made coders (and gamers) of our young. The home computer had arrived.

Running alongside the home computer was another class of device. The division wasn't distinct, but it was there. The 'school' computer was a little more expensive, and in the UK none were more present in classrooms than the BBC Micro.

Created by no less than the British Broadcasting Corporation, it was a best-of-class machine with a price to match, placing it out of reach of all but the most affluent households. Hence, it found its home in schools. The computer was closely supported by a broadcast tv programme *The Computer Programme*, transmitted on the BBC, in which presenter Chris Searle learnt all about the computer and coding, taking the viewers on the journey with him.

The BBC was even the centrepiece of one of the first instances of public 'hacking'. Ian McNaught-Davis and John Coll were demonstrating a modem live on 'Micro Live' when their screen was suddenly taken over by an uninvited visitor. Happily, this hacker was benign, and took the opportunity to display a poem, before disappearing back down the modem. Earlier that year, the public had been introduced to the idea of hacking in John Badham's *WarGames*, and now suddenly a marginal edutainment show on the BBC made it real.

Despite the visibility that smash-hit space-trading game Elite brought to the machine (at one point, there were more copies of Elite on sale than there were computers to play it on), the BBC

Micro (and its successor, the more commercially focussed Acorn Archimedes) ultimately proved financially unsustainable.

But what a contribution! Alongside the Sinclair, Commodore, Dragon, Atari, and Oric, this boxy piece of hardware naturalized and domesticated computers. With the trusted arm of a public-service broadcaster around it, the BBC Micro occupies a lasting place in the geek-nation's hearts and did its part to jump-start an industry.

▶ Right: The BBC Model B boasted a full-size keyboard.

▲ Above: The 'Welcome' manual included with the BBC computer.

Beasts
of Balance

#INFO

THE GAME WAS ORIGINALLY CALLED FABULOUS
BEASTS, BUT HAD TO CHANGE ITS NAME DUE TO
A RESEMBLANCE TO A CERTAIN MOVIE...

SOME OF THE PIECES ARE DESIGNED TO BE MORE
SLIPPERY THAN OTHERS.

EACH GAME CONTAINS 24 PIECES

YOU CAN DOWNLOAD THE 3D PRINT SOURCE FILES
FOR THE GAME PIECES FROM THEIR SITE AND
REMIX THE GAME.

PLINTH REQUIRES 3X 1.5V AA BATTERIES (NOT
INCLUDED)

In the early 21st century, videogames leapt out of the screen. It'd been happening for a while. We started using them to create parties where we could sing at the screen, play pretend plastic instruments, sometimes even dance around whilst being motion-captured. For decades it had seemed like they were constrained by the boundary of the screen, then it all changed.

The declining price of technologies such as NFC (Near Field Communication) and RFID (Radio Frequency Identification) made it possible to create objects that could be cheaply produced and read by sensors, for input into videogames themselves. Physical toys, that could be sensed by a computer but without the clumsy need for scanning barcodes or other such visual markers. With small pieces of information stored invisibly inside them, they could add a whole new layer of interaction into play. The means of interaction even got its own genre – 'toys to life'.

The first of these games to really break through into mainstream success was Toys for Bob's, 'Skylanders'. A core game was released, around which collectible character figures were also sold. In turn, these would add to the game experience. It was a smash-hit, as retailers awoke to the possibility of new, ongoing sales. In an industry that appeared to be constantly sliding further and further towards virtualization, with more and more games becoming download-only, this was a breath of commercial fresh air. New, physical objects that could be sold! The gold-rush started fast and within a few years both Disney and LEGO would release their own takes on this technology; however, both would be cancelled by 2017.

Beasts of Balance took a new approach, riding the momentum of a renaissance in board games and combining it with a studio staff pedigree of makers and independent developers. A 'digital tabletop hybrid family board game', funded by a Kickstarter crowd-funding programme, it was the first project by start-up Sensible Objects. Born from the culture of the maker and indie-game community, Sensible Objects have been fascinatingly transparent about how the game was designed and created. By sharing the production process on their site, they demonstrated how accessibly cheap micro-electronics and 3D printing technologies can be rapidly prototyped into a playable concept. An inspiring demonstration, it fused together Jenga and Skylanders into an altogether new kind of play.

▲ Above: Beasts of Balance game item detail.

▶ Right: Beasts of Balance retail packaging and game pieces.

012.

Bioshock
Xbox 360 faceplate

2007

You pre-ordered it as soon you could. You saved and saved until you had the money to buy it. You queued up for the midnight store opening to make sure you had it just as soon as possible. And you kept the receipt just in case anything went wrong. So, there's no doubt that this is your console and you've been playing it ever since.

But your console looks exactly the same as everybody else's. It would be nice if there was some way to distinguish yours from the millions of others that have been sold since you queued in the cold of the early hours all those months ago. Even if it distinguished it from the consoles your friends owned, that would be enough.

You put as much effort into selecting the case for your phone as most people do choosing the actual device itself. You have stickers on your laptop so you can tell which silver rectangle is yours and to show the world what a style-conscious individual you are. So, what about personalization for your game console? Sure, you could attach stickers, but you'd think there would be something more deliberate and lasting you could do.

That must have been exactly what Microsoft were thinking, when they

designed the Xbox 360 to have a removable faceplate. The whole front of the console comes off and can be replaced. You might think this is just to make it easier for your to get a new one if the original breaks, and certainly you can find replacement grey faceplates in stores and on online auction sites. But the real reason for the removable faceplate is to allow you to customize your console. To make it your console.

You really like Bioshock? Then why not show the world by transforming your 360 into a celebration of all things Rapture? All the system ports and slots remain available to use, with apertures and sprung doors. Most of all – with this particular faceplate – not only do you demonstrate your love of the game but also your commitment to it, as this was only available to those who pre-ordered Bioshock in the UK. So, this isn't just about personalization and making the console yours. This is also about demonstrating how dedicated a fan you really are.

Not every console manufacturer has been so keen to embrace customization in this way, and Microsoft stopped selling them after they didn't exactly set the world on

fire. However, with the 3DS, Nintendo has created plenty of opportunities for players to personalize their devices. With removable cover plates bearing geometric patterns, Splatoon splats, or the beaming visages of Toad, Princess and Mario, there are plenty of opportunities to make your 3DS your 3DS – and, of course, to spend more money in the process.

⊕INFO

ACCORDING TO MICROSOFT, ORIGINAL XBOX 360 CONSOLE FACEPLATES ARE:
· RESISTANT TO SCRATCHING AND FADING
· EASY TO CHANGE
· AVAILABLE IN LIMITED-EDITION DESIGNS

GUIDANCE ON REMOVING A FACEPLATE:
NOTE: YOU WILL NEED TO USE SOME FORCE TO REMOVE THE FACEPLATE

INSTRUCTIONS FOR FITTING A NEW FACEPLATE: ALIGN THE TABS ON THE FACEPLATE WITH THE SLOTS ON THE CONSOLE AND PRESS FIRMLY UNTIL THE FACEPLATE CLICKS INTO PLACE

▶ Right: Bioshock X-box 360 faceplate (front and rear).

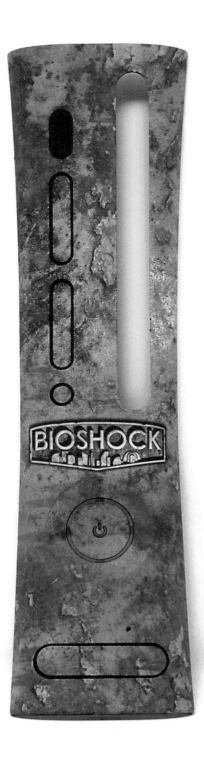

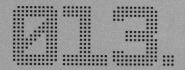

013.

Boktai:
The Sun Is In Your Hand

2003

#INFO

GENRE: ACTION ADVENTURE ROLE-PLAYING GAME
DEVELOPER: KONAMI COMPUTER ENTERTAINMENT JAPAN
PLAYER CHARACTER: DJANGO
PRINCIPAL WEAPON: GUN DEL SOL
FAMITSU REVIEW SCORE: 36 OUT OF 40
PRODUCER: HIDEO KOJIMA
WRITER AND DIRECTOR: IKUYA NAKAMURA

You are Django, a vampire hunter. And what's the one thing we know about vampires? That's right, they don't like garlic. OK, OK, what's the other thing we know about them? That's right, they just can't bear sunlight. Better equip yourself with your trusty Gun Del Sol and get to work.

Setting the date, time and time zone when starting allows the game to calculate the rising and setting of the sun in your location and adjust the in-game day accordingly. So far, so good. The game's world matches the player's world. But Boktai is hardly the first game to do that. In fact, so far, not much of what we've described distinguishes this 2003 Game Boy Advance title from any number of other Role Playing Games. However, Boktai has an important twist in its tail – or rather in its cartridge – that comes in the form of a photometric sensor.

What's a photometric sensor? It's a sensor that detects light. Sunlight. The sunlight that vampires hate. The sunlight that powers the Gun Del Sol. And where do you get sunlight from? Outside.

So, to charge up your vampire hunting weapon, you have go outside and soak up the rays – well, you need the cartridge to soak up the rays, so strictly speaking you can be smothered from head to toe in Factor

50 or even go back inside (which, incidentally, makes this game much easier to play if you happen to be a vampire yourself).

The light sensor is probably the thing that most obviously distinguishes Boktai from other Role Playing Games. The other is the way that the game-play requires you to sneak around without being detected rather than going in guns blazing and swords unsheathed. This might seem unusual for an RPG, but it all makes more sense when you discover that Boktai was worked on by Hideo Kojima, whose Metal Gear Solid

series is pretty much the epitome of stealth gaming.

So, if anybody tells you videogames just lead to people sitting around on sofas indoors all day and not getting enough fresh air and vitamin D, just hand them a copy of Boktai and tell them to go outside (while you sit on the sofa and bid on eBay for that copy of Boktai 2: Solar Boy Django or the Japanese-only Shin Bokura no Taiyo: Gyakushu no Sabata).

▲ Above : Game-play screenshot.
▶ Right: Boktai cartridge and packaging.

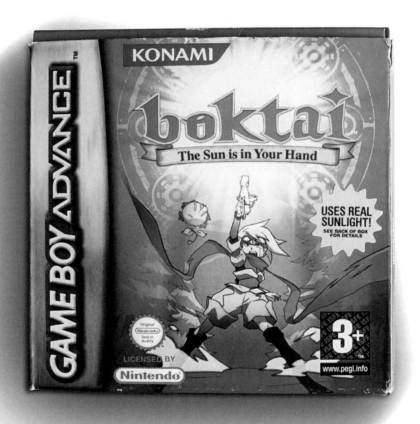

014

Buzz! Buzzers

2005

●INFO

'BUZZ!' SERIES DEVELOPED BY: RELENTLESS SOFTWARE
BUZZ! THE MUSIC QUIZ RELEASED: 2005
PLATFORM: PLAYSTATION 2
BUZZ VOICED BY: JASON DONOVAN
NUMBER OF BUZZ! BUZZERS SUPPLIED: 4
BUTTONS PER BUZZ! BUZZER: 5 (1 CIRCULAR RED BUTTON
WITH BLUE, ORANGE, GREEN AND YELLOW ANSWER
SELECTION BUTTONS)

Following the conspicuous success of EyeToy and the London Studio PlayStation 2 titles, videogames had accelerated their march across the living room. No longer were they about what happened on the screen, now you sang, danced, jumped about – had *parties* which were enabled by the games themselves. Party games, who'd have thought it?!

Of course, if you weren't using a microphone in singstar, or just leaping about in front of an eyetoy camera, the problem of the 'dualshock' controller remained. For these 'casual' titles, the default PlayStation controller remained a real challenge. It's an amazing piece of design for playing videogames with, but it's also very complicated to the uninitiated. With almost twenty buttons and two analogue sticks, if you don't already know about games, it doesn't offer the easiest on-ramp.

Relentless Software in Brighton found themselves with the opportunity to work on a quiz game in 2005. Acquiring the rights to a database of multiple-choice questions and inspired by the recent rush in party games, they set about thinking up a more accessible way to present a quiz to players. In order to create a party quiz game though, they needed

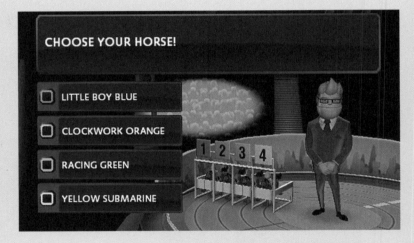

to find a way to engage up to four players at the same time. This couldn't be about adding more dualshock controllers, it had to be about a new kind of peripheral.

The brief they went out with, 'four buttons and a buzzer', led to a wide variety of prototypes being produced before they settled on the final design. A big red buzzer which illuminated when pressed became both an accessible, fun interface and the signature icon of the game. When stacked up at retail, it immediately read as a perfect family package. It couldn't help but stand out – perfectly, obviously, the Buzz Buzzer.

▲ Above: Buzz! game screenshot and retail packaging.

▶ Right: Set of four Buzz! Buzzer controllers.

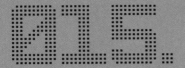

015.
Commodore 64
1982

#INFO

DEVELOPMENT CODENAME: VIC40
UNITS SOLD: 10—17 MILLION
RAM: 65,536 BYTES (64 KILOBYTES)
MAIN PROCESSORS: MOS6502 (CPU),
VIC-II (GRAPHICS), SID (SOUND)
ORIGINAL RETAIL PRICE: $595

In 1982, Commodore Business Machines released a machine that changed the world of videogaming forever. The machine in question was the Commodore 64 (more commonly known as the C64 or CBM64 to its many fans) and it would go on to become the bestselling home computer of all time, with somewhere between 10–17 million units sold. But how did it transform gaming?

Partly, it was about the price ($495 might seem like a lot, but in 1982 this was a comparatively inexpensive computer) and partly it was due to the fact that you could buy a C64 in ordinary retailers rather than only in specialist computer stores like its rivals.

But mostly the C64's success was down to its specification. The C64 was an 8-bit home computer with 64 kilobytes of RAM and a processor running at roughly 1MHz. Its graphics processor was capable of displaying 16 colours (though not necessarily all at the same time, depending on the screen resolution which was set between 160x200 and 320x200 pixels). These capabilities might seem pretty unimpressive by today's standards but in 1982 this was pretty high-end stuff. It might be surprising to find a gaming machine released by a business machine manufacturer (we should remember that the PCs that

run all those First Person Shooters were originally designed for spreadsheets and word processors, too). In fact, part of the reason for the C64's sophisticated graphics capabilities was to enable the machine to be used to create complex charts and graphs for high-powered executives to showcase their company profits in boardrooms. But once programmers got hold of the machine, they soon realized that Commodore had accidentally created a gaming super-platform.

It wasn't all about the graphics, either. The C64 also included a sound chip that blew every other computer's out of the water because it was designed by somebody who knew about music and wasn't content with out-of-tune beeping noises. You can read more about the SID chip on page 178.

Before long, spreadsheets and pie charts were forgotten and, all over the

world, C64's were being used to play games like Impossible Mission, Monty on the Run and Thing on a Spring. This was despite the fact that games were distributed on cassettes that took many minutes to load (later in the C64's life, programmers worked out how to include 'loading music', graphics and even mini games to keep players amused while the main game was loading).

Ironically, when Commodore released the C64 Games System (C64GS) in 1990 as a more streamlined, cartridge-based competitor to the Nintendo Entertainment System, it was such a flop that it was never released outside Europe.

Today, the C64 remains a popular computer for enthusiasts, retro gamers and musicians With numerous emulators in production and games available via the Nintendo eStore, for example.

◀ Far left: The original packaging.

▲ Above: The original Commodore 64 was known as the 'breadbin'.

◀ Left: Detail of keyboard showing the graphic symbols that can be entered.

016.

Commodore
Amiga 500 (Golden)

1987

#INFO

DEVELOPMENT CODENAME: ROCK LOBSTER
RELEASED: 1987
ORIGINAL PRICE: $699/£499
CPU: MOTOROLA 6800
ORIGINAL CHIP SET: AGNUS (CONTROLLER),
DENISE (GRAPHICS), PAULA (SOUND)
STANDARD CASE COLOUR: BEIGE

Compared with most of the home computers that preceded it, the Commodore Amiga has a lot in common with modern-day machines. Where a lot of previous systems had relied on text input, the Amiga was built from the ground up to be an audiovisual powerhouse. It was a multimedia computer before there were multimedia computers. There's a graphical user interface (GUI), a mouse that you point and click with. The system can multitask, which means it can run multiple applications at the same time. The Commodore 64 had been wildly successful, but the Amiga was a step up. This was definitely a grown-up computer and its graphics and sound capabilities meant that it ended up seeing use in certain professional settings, performing video editing, captioning and titling duties.

One area where the value of its advanced audiovisual capabilities was immediately spotted was in games. With the ability to play back four channels of samples, via its 'PAULA' chip, Amiga music sounded different to the chip tunes of 8-bit computers – or consoles, like the NES. Combine the enhanced sound with more memory and full-colour graphics, and the Amiga was almost perfect for game development. Like the C64 before it, the Amiga emerged as an extremely important (but now often overlooked) gaming platform.

The list of Amiga developers reads like a *Who's Who* of the industry: Sensible Software released the still much-loved Sensible Soccer and Cannon Fodder; Team 17 launched Worms into the world; the Bitmap Brothers crafted fiendishly difficult and almost impossibly good looking shoot-em-ups like Xenon and futuristic sports games such as Speedball; and DMA Design created titles like Lemmings, which saw the player guide a band of hapless creatures seemingly determined to meet their own demise. DMA would go on to create a certain Grand Theft Auto. This really was a crucible of talent.

Eric Chahi's Another World brought a fluidity of animation and lavish cut-scenes that would go on to inspire developers seeking to combine cinematic spectacle and storytelling with rich game-play. In the US, LucasArts brought their groundbreaking point-and-click adventures like Loom and The Secret of Monkey Island to the system.

There were a number of different Amiga models released during the platform's 1985–1996 lifespan. It all began with the Amiga 1000 and ended with the extremely powerful 1200, but it was the Amiga 500 that

really hit the sweet spot of price and performance. The gold-cased Amiga 500 pictured here commemorates the one millionth machine produced, as evidenced by the illustrated certificate of authenticity.

What is interesting is that the Amiga was so far ahead of its time that it is only in recent years that the true scale of its innovations is being understood. It wasn't just that the Amiga was a multimedia computer before there were multimedia computers. The Amiga was a multimedia computer before there was multimedia.

▲ Above : Close-up of the disk drive.

◤ Right (above): Certificate of authenticity.

▶ Right : The millionth Commodore Amiga 500.

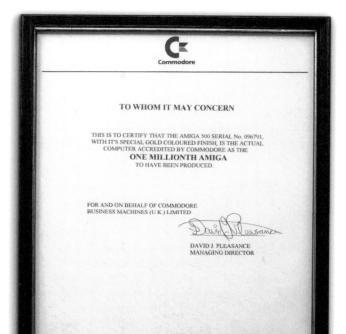

TO WHOM IT MAY CONCERN

THIS IS TO CERTIFY THAT THE AMIGA 500 SERIAL No. 096791,
WITH IT'S SPECIAL GOLD COLOURED FINISH, IS THE ACTUAL
COMPUTER ACCREDITED BY COMMODORE AS THE
ONE MILLIONTH AMIGA
TO HAVE BEEN PRODUCED.

FOR AND ON BEHALF OF COMMODORE
BUSINESS MACHINES (U.K.) LIMITED

DAVID J. PLEASANCE
MANAGING DIRECTOR

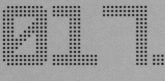

CRT
TV
1988

+INFO

CRT TV FIRST DEMONSTRATED BY KENJIRO TAKAYANAGI IN 1925
FIRST COMMERCIALLY AVAILABLE CRT TV SETS SOLD IN
GERMANY IN 1935 BY TELEFUNKEN
LARGEST SIZE OF CRT DISPLAY: 38—40 INCHES
DESIGNATION OF CRTS BY UNITED STATES ENVIRONMENTAL
PROTECTION AGENCY (EPA): 'HAZARDOUS HOUSEHOLD WASTE'
LAST SALES OF CRT TVS IN THE UK BY LARGEST ELECTRICAL
RETAILER DSG: 2006

Aren't modern TVs great? So big. So bright. So wide.

There was a time when a 21" screen would have been considered to be large, and the pin-sharp ultra HD resolutions of today's massive, wall-filling displays weren't even feasible in science fiction. There was a time when TV sets had curved glass fronts that distorted the picture and made it look like you were watching everything through a goldfish bowl. That already-bowed picture looked blurry and slightly out-of-focus, and every time something moved on screen it left behind it a ghostly afterimage. If you got right up close to the TV, you could see the horizontal lines of little red, green and blue dots that made up the picture. In fact, you didn't need to get that close to see them, as they were pretty visible. Those small, blurry screens were what we plugged our videogame consoles into.

That was less than 20 years ago and, although it sounds terrible, not only did we not know any different, but those consoles were designed for those TVs, and game creators took advantage of the way images were displayed and mangled. Which means that games from the 1980s and 1990s often look worse on modern LCD televisions than they do on old-fashioned Cathode Ray Tube sets.

But how can that be? Curved glass and distorted low resolution images sound dreadful. Perhaps this is just nostalgia, a yearning for the past and a desire to cling onto the stuff from childhood? Are we just convincing ourselves that old TVs look better? Like when people tell you vinyl sounds better than CDs? There may be a bit of nostalgia in there and certainly the sheer size of an old set gives it an imposing presence in any living room or bedroom. But, there really is something in the claim that a 1980s or 1990s videogame might look better on a 1980s or 1990s TV set.

The reason is pretty simple. Game developers used the imperfections of CRTs to create visual effects and cover some of the limitations of early graphics hardware. One famous example is Activision's Atari 2600 racing game Enduro. Play it on a modern LCD and the racing car's wheels look as though they have spikes coming out of them. It's like driving a chariot from Ben Hur. Play the game on a CRT and the blurriness of the display smoothes out the graphics and you get an effect that looks like the tyres spinning. Play Goldeneye 007 on a modern LCD and you'll likely notice the polygons have jagged edges. Switch to a CRT and they're magically gone. Or magically blurred away, anyway.

Of course, some modern videogame emulators also simulate the effects of these imperfections and let players activate scan lines and blurriness. But, for retrogamers after the most authentic experience, that N64 just has to be plugged into a massive fishbowl of a CRT. And, with modern LCD TVs doing away with analogue audiovisual connections like SCART, S-Video and good old RF in favour of digital connections like HDMI, a CRT is often not just the best option, but possibly the only option.

▲ Above: Ferguson CRT TV SCART socket (PAL version).

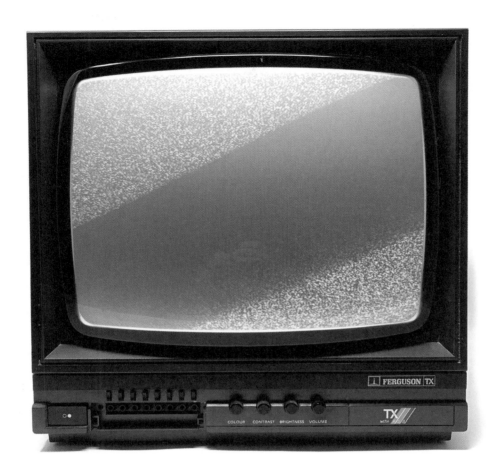

▲ Above: Ferguson CRT TV (PAL version) with details including Sonic 2 stickers (peeling).

018.

Dance:UK
dancemat

2003

◆INFO

DIMENSIONS: 34.5 X 30.5 X 11.7 CM
NUMBER OF BUTTONS: UP, DOWN, LEFT,
RIGHT, SQUARE, CIRCLE, TRIANGLE, CROSS,
START, SELECT

Music and videogames have always been inextricably linked. Think of your favourite game and as well as the graphics and action, your brain has almost certainly started replaying the soundtrack, which is now bobbing away in the background. Music makes videogames come to life. Sometimes, as with Mario or Sonic, it's an irresistibly catchy tune that just works its way into your brain and captures the rhythm and tempo of the action. Sometimes, as with Metal Gear Solid or Skyrim, it's an epic, orchestral score that builds tension and drama. And sometimes, like with Rez or Parappa the Rapper, it just makes you want to dance. But that can be a bit of a problem. Videogames also require precision and so, when faced with getting Parappa's kicks and punches perfectly timed, getting up and busting some moves on the living room carpet is unlikely to help.

What you need is a game where it doesn't matter so much if you're dancing around. In fact, what you need is a game where dancing around is a positively good idea. A game you controlled by dancing around. Somebody should invent a dancemat. Oh, that's right, they did. As early as 1986, Bandai released the Family Trainer (also known as the Family Fitness Trainer and the Power Pad in Europe and the US). The focus here was more on exercise through jogging and aerobics than on dancing per se, but the idea of a floor mat with buttons operated by the feet was firmly established.

The dancemat as we are more familiar with it today typically takes the form of a 3 x 3 grid with a central position, left, right, up and down, and diagonal buttons that roughly equate with the eight directional positions of a joypad or joystick. Dancemats come in hard and soft varieties, with the former more usually seen in arcades, and the latter in the home, where they can be rolled up and stored when not in use.

Konami's Dance Dance Revolution (DDR) series is probably the most well known, and was largely responsibly for popularizing the 'beatmania' (or Bemani as it's abbreviated in Japan) of rhythm and dance games. Over the years, there have been Disney-themed versions of DDR along with Mario, Hello Kitty and even Winnie the Pooh themed special editions.

While music games such as Guitar Hero and Rock Band fell from favour and all but disappeared after a period of intense popularity in the mid-2000s, dancing games remain popular, with Ubisoft's Just Dance series available for contemporary

consoles. And if you want to see some truly masterful moves, visit a Game Center in Tokyo's Akihabara district. Entire floors of these arcades are dedicated to dancing games, often with machines linked together so that multiple dancers can perform their well-practised, choreographed and synchronized routines. Leaping between machines is all part of the performance, even if it has no effect on the game. But, the dancemat isn't only about what's happening on screen or getting a perfect score. It's about spectacle and performance in the real world. It's show business.

▲ Above: Detail of 'Up' control.

▶ Right: Detail of dancemat (PlayStation version).

019.

The
Dark Wheel

1984

In the last few decades, videogames have been obsessed with being cinematic. High-Definition, 4K, ultra-real, motion-captured performances thrill us, move us, and attempt to be indistinguishable from their Hollywood counterparts. Several decades earlier, when the polygon count of an entire videogame might be less than one, the aspirations were very different. Videogames were a place for stories, for adventure, perhaps even literature in and of themselves.

The work of developers like Infocom with their 'interactive fiction' projects carved out a new territory for videogames as complex, long-form pieces of playable fiction. Within this genre, two notable examples took established books and adapted them into a playable format. Infocom's The Hitchhiker's Guide to the Galaxy and Melbourne House's The Hobbit both adapted much-loved stories into new, playable worlds. In 1984, for the first time in videogames, the dynamic was reversed.

World-Building is hard. Creating an apparently persistent, believable universe in which the player can explore, make their own decisions,

and have their own agency was remarkably executed in a game called 'Elite'. A space-trading game which took place in a vast universe, it delivered a scale and scope never seen before. So big, in fact, that it was able to accommodate the imaginative breadth of a novella.

While it was commissioned as a marketing device, adding value to the pack-in materials alongside the game in the box, 'The Dark Wheel' was more than that. A short piece of literary science-fiction created by the then up-and-coming writer Robert Holdstock, the inclusion of the novella with the game insisted that this was something more than the usual. This was a game with a universe big enough to accommodate a novella.

Contemporary videogames aspire to this frequently, often commissioning writers to create an extended universe of stories to colour in the World around the IP of their core game, for sale separately to die-hard fans.

Elite delivered something provocatively different. In shipping the novella with the game it announced that it was distinct, literate, deeper. The game, the novella, the universe – all in the box.

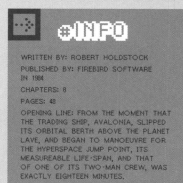

●INFO

WRITTEN BY: ROBERT HOLDSTOCK
PUBLISHED BY: FIREBIRD SOFTWARE
IN 1984
CHAPTERS: 8
PAGES: 48
OPENING LINE: FROM THE MOMENT THAT THE TRADING SHIP, AVALONIA, SLIPPED ITS ORBITAL BERTH ABOVE THE PLANET LAVE, AND BEGAN TO MANOEUVRE FOR THE HYPERSPACE JUMP POINT, ITS MEASUREABLE LIFE-SPAN, AND THAT OF ONE OF ITS TWO-MAN CREW, WAS EXACTLY EIGHTEEN MINUTES.

▲ Above: Screenshot of game.

◀ Right (clockwise from top): ZX Spectrum Elite retail packaging; cardboard keyboard overlap; 'The Dark Wheel' novella; Game manual.

Dizzy III
development map
1989

HAND-DRAWN IN PENCIL BY PHILIP AND ANDREW OLIVER
DIZZY III IS THE DEVELOPMENT NAME FOR FANTASY WORLD
DIZZY, RELEASED IN 1989 BY CODEMASTERS
MAP GRID: 8 X 16 SQUARES/SCREENS
ANNOTATIONS INCLUDE: 'CAKE' AND 'DAGGER'
SQUARE 109 IS MYSTERIOUSLY BLANK!

It's fair to say that the Oliver Twins know a thing or two about making videogames. Philip and Andrew began writing games when they were still at school in Trowbridge, England. Throughout their career, they have sold millions of games, and had no fewer than ten UK chart-topping hits. They were so prolific and so popular that in the mid-1980s it was reported that seven per cent of all games sold in the UK were theirs. Among their best-loved creations is Dizzy. A lovable egg with arms, legs, a winning smile and a somersaulting jump, Dizzy and the other members of the Yolkfolk (the Olivers were also not afraid of some egg-based wordplay) were staples of 1980s home computer gaming.

Confusingly, even though it was called Dizzy III in development, Fantasy World Dizzy as it was eventually titled wasn't actually the third Dizzy game to be released. That honour, in fact, goes to 'Fast Food', a spin-off from the main Dizzy series that saw everybody's favourite egg racing round a maze that looked just a bit like that belonging to a certain yellow munching character also inspired by a foodstuff. Let's hope the two never met up – a tasty-looking egg and a mobile mouth that just wants to consume everything in its path. It doesn't bear thinking about.

But, back to Dizzy III. Like the previous titles in the main Dizzy series, this was a platform game with action adventure elements and an emphasis on puzzle solving. The game world was divided into a number of 'screens', each with a given name and each containing specific items, characters or obstacles to be used or overcome in order to make progress.

The game was designed on paper – squared paper – with each of the individual screens literally mapped out by hand in pencil. Every screenful of game-play was meticulously designed, drawn, and reworked before being translated into bits and bytes and leaping into life as computer code. And so the pencil marks on these carefully numbered map sections were translated into computer graphics. Marks on the page became light on the screen. Graph paper became pixels. For a game about an ovoid, there sure were a lot of squares involved.

The Dizzy III development map tells us a lot about the process of making games in the 1980s, and the amount of planning and preparation that went on in the analogue world before the game took digital form. But it isn't just a matter of converting the sketches into code. Playing through the game with the map alongside, it is possible to see where certain puzzles or the layout of

certain screens has been altered. Similarly, the magic of code means that if Dizzy needs to fall down a deep well, only one shaft needs to be drawn and it can be looped, thereby saving previous memory and resources.

And how did the Olivers translate their pencil designs into Amstrad CPC code? Perhaps they used the many tools available for creating animation routines and character graphics? Not exactly. In the absence of commercially available development tools, they did what all entrepreneurial coding experts would do, and created their own. Panda Sprites was one such package and was used to simplify the process of creating animation.

Wondering about the name Panda Sprites? 'Sprite' refers to the name used in computing for character graphics (as distinct from background elements). So, Dizzy is a sprite (and also an egg). But what about Panda? Surely a program that specializes in creating animations of bamboo-eating bears could only have a limited appeal? In fact, that part of the name comes from the Olivers themselves: Philip and Andrew – P and A.

Yes, the Olivers definitely like word play, and they certainly know a thing or two about videogames. In fact, you might even say they have them cracked.

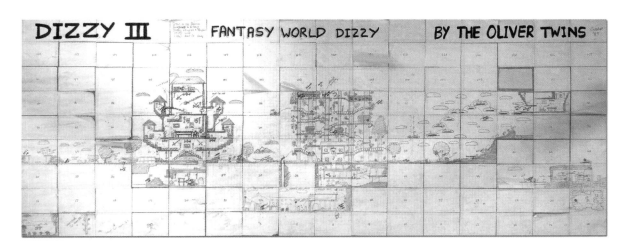

▲ Above: Hand-drawn Dizzy III development map (top); map details and screenshot.

021.

Donkey Kong
Arcade Cabinet

1981

●INFO

PRODUCER: GUNPEI YOKOI
DIRECTOR: SHIGERU MIYAMOTO
COIN-OP CABINET RELEASED: 1981
BASED ON: RADAR SCOPE HARDWARE
CPU: ZILOG Z80 AT 3.072 MHZ
MONITOR ORIENTATION: VERTICAL
DISPLAY RESOLUTION: 224 X 256 PIXELS
INSPIRED BY: KING KONG, BEAUTY AND THE BEAST
HIGH SCORE: 1,218,000 (WES COPELAND, 5 MAY 2016)

Like many coin-op manufacturers, Nintendo had been trying to break into the US market for some time, and in 1980 their latest unsuccessful attempt had left the company with a large number of unsold Radar Scope machines. The cross between Space Invaders and Galaxian had been popular in Japan, but its success hadn't translated as hoped. Attempting to salvage the situation, Nintendo of Japan's Chief Executive Officer Hiroshi Yamauchi challenged his developers to come up with a new design that made use of the languishing Radar Scope hardware. The winner of the competition was a certain Shigeru Miyamoto and the game he proposed would go on to become Donkey Kong. Conversion kits were made up and shipped to America and 2000 Radar Scope machines were transformed – as was the videogame industry. Nintendo's fortunes went up and up, just like... you get the idea.

Donkey Kong is a platform game which sees the titular ape perched atop a building site throwing a multitude of objects including barrels and springs at our intrepid hero who, as everybody knows, is called Mario. Except that he isn't.

You mean Mario isn't a hero? No, Mario's always the hero, right. It's just that this isn't Mario, because in the original Japanese Donkey Kong game the lead character was actually called Jumpman. That's not a bad name really for a character that spends most of their time running and jumping (with some occasional climbing thrown in for good measure). So, not Mario but Jumpman. In fact, if you really want to get detailed about it, Miyamoto had originally wanted to call him Mr Video. In fact, if you really want to get even more detailed about it, Miyamoto actually wanted to build the game around characters from the Popeye cartoon, but Nintendo weren't able to secure the license.

And talking of licenses, Universal Studios soon got wind of this popular game and started to wonder whether the 'Donkey Kong' name might be an infringement of their 'King Kong' property. Slugging it out in court, Nintendo won and the rest is history.

But, where did that name come from? Why 'Donkey' Kong? Over the years, there have been a lot of different explanations and urban myths including one claiming that a bad phone line meant a translator misheard the games actual name of 'Monkey Kong'. Miyamoto himself says that 'Donkey' was meant to refer to the silly stubbornness of the

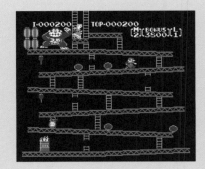

character which, although more believable, isn't quite as exciting a story.

Oh, and remember when we said before that Mario was always a hero? Well, that's not exactly true. In 1982's Donkey Kong Jr., Mario wasn't running anywhere and he certainly wasn't jumping. Instead, DK Jr. did all the hard work leaping and climbing vines. Why's that you ask? Because he was trying to rescue his Papa from the clutches of the evil... wait for it... Mario! It's the one and only time Mario was the villain of the piece. Be honest, you always half suspected he had it in him, right?

▲ Above: Game-play screen shot from the first level.

▶ Right: This recreated Donkey Kong cabinet includes the artwork decals but omits the coin slots.

Dragon User magazine type-in code listing

1983

#INFO

MAGAZINE: DRAGON USER
COVER PRICE: 60P
PUBLISHED BY: SUNSHINE BOOKS DRAGON AND ITS
LOGO TRADEMARKED BY DRAGON DATA LTD
BUST-OUT, COPYRIGHT 1983, G. SINGH

One of the defining features of a videogame console is that it is a closed system. If you want to create games for an NES or PlayStation, you need to register as a developer and use the special programming and debugging tools like the ones on pages 138-139. There's no easy way for the ordinary console owner to tinker with, modify or create their own original games.

That's where computers differ. They're programmable, meaning that the user most definitely can get under the hood and start experimenting with code. Indeed, the promise of home computers in the 1980s was that everybody would become a programmer. There were books teaching the fundamentals of BASIC and describing advanced machine code techniques. There were television programmes like the BBC's *Micro Live* in the UK that aimed to help the uninitiated distinguish between a floppy disk and a printer. And there were magazines. And those magazines probably had CDs on the front with demos and examples? Well, yes, by the mid-1990s, magazines like the *Official PlayStation Magazine* had CD cover discs. But before then? Cassettes? Occasionally, yes, but those were expensive to duplicate and

fragile to ship out to newsagents. So, in the very earliest days, computing magazines printed out listings of code. Long listings of code. Readers would type in this code and execute it on their computer whereupon the program would run.

Maybe.

Because, of course, there's a lot that could go wrong. The user might very easily transcribe the code incorrectly. One mistyped character would bring the whole program grinding to an unceremonious halt with a 'Syntax Error'. OK, check the code in the magazine. Check the code you've typed in matches. Sometimes, it was simple: a 1 that should have been a 0, a line that was skipped in the excitement to get the code entered. But sometimes, these bug hunts were altogether harder – maybe even impossible. Sometimes, the code was printed incorrectly in the magazine. What possible chance could you have? Well, in fact, for some readers this really helped them learn to code. Once they'd established that they'd copied everything correctly, the task shifted to debugging, which involved really understanding what the different routines and sub-routines were supposed to be doing. For

everybody else, there was an agonizing wait until next month's issue and the printout of the corrections to the incorrect code – ah, that should have been >1 not <1.

The listings pictured here come from *Dragon User* magazine, which was published in the early 1980s. Each month, the magazine would print code listings for utilities and games that could be run on the Dragon 32 home computer. To help would-be coders understand the programs, each listing had accompanying notes that explained what each section of the code did – initializing values, printing on-screen instructions, checking and updating the score.

Ironically, given how susceptible media such as floppy disks and CDs are to deterioration over time and how easily they stop working, these code listings printed on paper actually have a pretty good shelf-life, and are likely to be around long into the future.

▶ Right (top): 'Bust-out!' code listing from Dragon User magazine; (bottom) Detail of code listings.

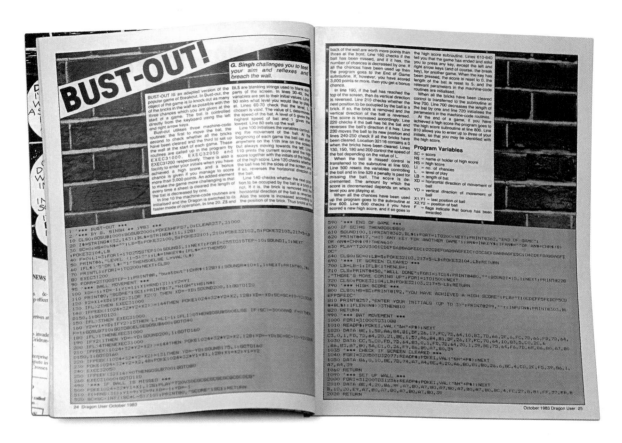

Dreamcast Visual Memory Unit (VMU)

1998

Over the years, there have been a number of different approaches to the problem of saving game progress. In the earliest days, games such as Nintendo's Metroid used often complex password systems which eventually gave way to battery-backed memory in cartridges such as The Legend of Zelda. Once CDs and DVDs made writing to the disc impossible, Sony, Microsoft and Nintendo used removable mini cartridges for PlayStations, Xboxes and GameCubes. Meanwhile, SNK had been using PCMCIA cards since the 1990s that allowed players to continue game-play started in the arcade on their home Neo Geo systems and vice versa. The impact on game design was pretty significant as, since they did not need to be completable in a single sitting, games could be longer – they could have more complex stories that unfolded after days, weeks or even months of play. But, regardless of the technology, all of these systems set out to perform the same basic job: let you save your game part way through so you could pick it up again later. Given the world of videogaming's love of innovation and invention, it is surprising how little the memory card changed over the years.

Until the Dreamcast, that is, and the launch of the Visual Memory Unit. The VMU, as it was colloquially known, is first and foremost a game-save cartridge. As the Dreamcast used read-only optical discs as its primary distribution media, some form of writable memory was required. So far so unremarkable. However, the VMU's ability to save game progress or character stats are far and away its least interesting features. Let's look more carefully at the device. It doesn't really look like a memory card. It has an LCD for displaying monochrome graphics, sound capabilities, a D-Pad, and A and B buttons. It almost looks like a mini console. Which is precisely what it is.

Certain Dreamcast titles included mini-games that could be downloaded to the VMU and played separate to the main attraction. Sonic Adventure's Chao Adventure virtual pet mini game allowed players to hatch a little creature on the VMU which, once trained to be stronger and faster, could be introduced back into the Dreamcast game. There were even multiplayer and data transfer options as VMUs could be linked together via the connector on the top of the unit.

But it's more than a mini console. The VMU could also act as a second screen. In games such as Dino Crisis the VMU showed data about the player's health while in sports games like those in the NFL 2K series the VMU allowed players in multiplayer games to select plays without their opponent seeing. This was very much the forerunner of the Wii U's asymmetric multiplayer gaming, as seen in NintendoLand's Animal Crossing: Sweet Day and Mario Chase. A short while after the VMU was launched, Sony added the PocketStation hybrid memory card/ mini console to the PlayStation line-up, though it was never released outside Japan.

⊙INFO

PROCESSOR: SANYO LC8670
POWER: 2 X CR2032 LITHIUM BATTERIES (INCLUDES AUTO POWER OFF)
DISPLAY: LCD (48 X 32 PIXELS)
DISPLAY SIZE: 37 X 26MM
DEVICE DIMENSIONS (W, H, D): 47MM X 80MM X 16 MM
SPECIAL EDITIONS: GODZILLA, HELLO KITTY, SONIC THE HEDGEHOG

◀ Right (top): Dreamcast VMU unit.

▶ Right (bottom): Screenshots from Dreamcast VMU 'Street Race'.

 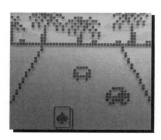 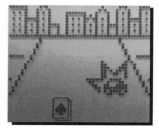

024.
E.T. the Extra-Terrestrial
Atari 2600 cartridge
1982

INFO

DESIGNED BY: HOWARD SCOTT WARSHAW
RELEASED: DECEMBER 1982
GAME DEVELOPED IN: 5 AND A HALF WEEKS
FEE FOR RIGHT TO E.T. LICENSE:
$20-25 MILLION
TOTAL NUMBER OF ATARI CARTRIDGES
BURIED IN 1983: 728,000

Over the years, the Atari 2600 game E.T. The Extra Terrestrial has got a pretty bad rap. It has become commonplace in videogame history to almost single-handedly blame it for the 1983 US market crash. The story goes that Atari were so certain that the game would follow the astronomical success of the film that they actually manufactured more E.T. cartridges than the number of Atari 2600 consoles they'd currently sold. The idea was that people would want to play the game so much that they would go and buy a 2600 to do so. And that's why Atari reportedly paid somewhere between $20–25 million for the license. It was a guaranteed winner. Videogames were fantastically popular, E.T. was the hottest film in town, the 1982 holidays season was approaching. How could it fail?

Well, how about giving the programmer, Howard Scott Warshaw, just a few months to complete the game? How about ignoring Spielberg's suggestions for the game's design? How about not conducting any audience play-testing before the release? Yes, that could help it fail. In fact, it sounds like a recipe for disaster. And that's exactly what happened.

If we fast forward to gory details of the poor reviews, even poorer sales, and the lines of players who did purchase the title waiting to

disappointedly return it, and cut to Alamogordo in New Mexico, we find lorry-loads of cartridges being dumped in a landfill site. Why bury them? Basically, it was considered that getting rid of them made more economic sense than storing them or trying to sell them in such a hostile market. So, from the 1982 excitement and anticipation of the biggest title in videogame history to a 1983 mass cartridge burial, we see how quickly fortunes can turn. And that's the story of Atari 2600 E.T.

Except it isn't really the full story, and it does pretty much lay the blame for the entire US market crash at the feet of one game, which isn't really fair.

Let's be clear. E.T. is not a great game, and Atari did gamble an awful lot on it selling well, which it clearly didn't. Ironically, it's actually become quite a popular title now, but that's as much because of its notoriety as any game-play features. Copies extracted from the desert often fetch disproportionately high prices on eBay.

But, even though players were left unimpressed by E.T., it was far from the only underwhelming game in the early 1980s, and US consumers didn't turn their back on the entirety of videogaming just because of one bad cartridge.

Atari had already had a near-miss with its 2600 conversion of Pac-Man,

which received harsh critical reviews despite selling well – less than anticipated, but well nonetheless. Worse than that, though, was the sheer number of titles being churned out for the system. Purina's Chase the Chuck Wagon holds the dubious title of being the first videogame about dog food. There's probably a reason that most people have never heard of it, and it's probably the same reason why it's also, as far as we know, the only videogame about dog food.

In Japan, they call the 1983 US market crash 'Atari Shock', which is a bit kinder than blaming it all on E.T.

▲ An original Atari 2600 screenshot from E.T.: The Extra-Terrestrial.

▶ Right: Original packaging and cartridge from the most-pulped game in history (PAL version).

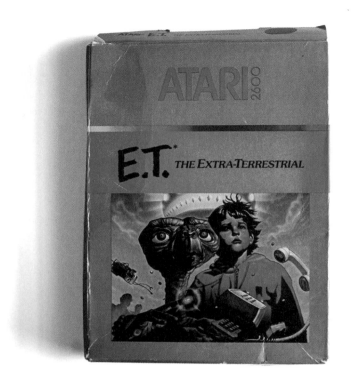

025.
EDGE magazine
issue 1
1993

Since the earliest days of home computers, magazines have been essential reading for gamers. Before the Internet and comparatively easy access to previews and features about forthcoming games; before the plethora of YouTube Let's Play that don't just show you snippets of gameplay but tour you through the experience in its entirety, side-quests and all; and before Twitter made it possible to follow game developers, see their work in progress and get regular updates on new features; before all of this immediate, on-demand access to rich information, there was print.

Magazine adverts helped keen players discover new releases while reviews helped them spend their money wisely by nominating the best games for plaudits and identifying those best avoided. Early game magazines carried code listings to type in new games. Later, cassettes and eventually CDs and DVDs were added as cover-mounted extras. There were videos of forthcoming games, playable demos, and even entirely free games. It got to the point where the cover-mounted goodies were almost more important than the written contents of the magazine. It was sometimes as if the magazine existed simply to provide something onto which the CD could be stuck.

It would be a brave decision to launch a magazine with no cover mount at all. Braver still would be to launch a magazine with lofty intentions, a desire to elevate the discussion of videogames and to contribute to a new language of games criticism. In 1993, Future Publishing bit the bullet and launched *Edge* with not a cover mount in sight.

What was immediately striking about *Edge* – and remains striking today – is the extraordinarily high production values. Heavyweight paper, a meticulous attention to typographical detail and page layout lent *Edge* the look and feel of a fashion or style journal rather than a games magazine. The cover alone was a work of art, with a single dominant image contrasting with the busy, visual cacophony of competing publications. Where they shouted for attention, *Edge* had the confidence to be measured, subtle. It knew you were interested in what it had to say. Part of the reason it could be so assured was that readers had to work hard to even find a copy. You couldn't buy *Edge* just anywhere. Initial distribution was comparatively limited and, better still, when you did find it on a shelf, it was impenetrably sealed in a plastic bag. If you wanted to glimpse the future of videogames, get a sneak peak at what was topping

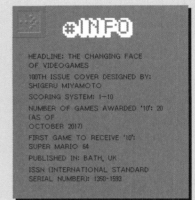

#INFO

HEADLINE: THE CHANGING FACE OF VIDEOGAMES
100TH ISSUE COVER DESIGNED BY: SHIGERU MIYAMOTO
SCORING SYSTEM: 1–10
NUMBER OF GAMES AWARDED '10': 20 (AS OF OCTOBER 2017)
FIRST GAME TO RECEIVE '10': SUPER MARIO 64
PUBLISHED IN: BATH, UK
ISSN (INTERNATIONAL STANDARD SERIAL NUMBER): 1350-1593

the charts in Japan, you couldn't flick through the magazine in the store, you had to buy it. This was a commitment.

Over the years, *Edge* has continued to buck the trend of gaming magazines. In the face of the challenge of the web, YouTube, Twitter and the like, *Edge* continues to be a flagship publication, respected by players and the development community alike. Perhaps only Famitsu's reviews carry more weight and, like that esteemed tome, *Edge* awards its maximum review score only infrequently, Since 1993, only 20 titles have received the coveted '*Edge* 10'. The first came in 1996 with Super Mario 64 and most recently Super Mario Odyssey took the crown – or should that be Cappy?

The **future** of **video**gaming

October 1993 £three ¥900 $ten

EDGE

Mega Drive ■ Super Nintendo ■ **PC** ■ Amiga ■ **PC Engine** ■ Neo Geo ■ **3DO**

The changing face

of video **games**

3DO how the
dream machine
shapes up
in **real** life

1
Issue **one**

One of the animation frames from Psygnosis' CD-ROM
game, *Microcosm* (see page 70). Rendered in 3D using
Silicon Graphics workstations, the game uses 44,000
such images – a vast 298 megabytes' worth on one CD

9 771350 159007

▲ *Edge* magazine issue 1 (October 1993).

Electronic Arts'
We See Farther Advertisment

1983

It's often not apparent from looking at their packaging, but videogames are created by people. Trust us on this. One of the odd differences between games and other creative media in recent decades has been the absence of celebration (or even communication) of that fact. With a few notable exceptions, the presence of creators in the public life of videogames has been sadly lacking. Thankfully, the emergence of an independent sector of games development, with different marketing goals, is starting to repair that.

Back in the 1980s, when games were filled with an experimental confidence they wouldn't regain for years, a particularly challenging full-page advertisement ran in game magazines. We haven't seen anything like it since. A fledgling company called 'Electronic Arts' was making a bold statement. Under the title 'software artists?' was a beautifully shot, high-contrast, monochrome group portrait of some people. These people weren't being presented as awkward geeks, they hadn't ambled into the frame to be captured in their working scruffs.

They'd been art-directed, they were posed, they were here to be celebrated and to request your respect.

Surrounding them in the page layout were the specially commissioned artworks for each of their games. Often when one stands in a videogame store and looks at the shelves you could be forgiven for thinking you're looking at hundreds of copies of the same game. The glaring similarities in covers between every title can almost make them blur into one. These were different. Created in the square ratio of a vinyl album cover, each with a distinct art direction, they shouted out the individuality of each game. Not only that, but each bore the name of the developers proudly under the title.

Most wonderfully, despite the bold photography, the copy itself is disarmingly balanced. After the bold stand first of 'Software artists?' comes a tentative rebuff from one of the stars, Bill Budge: "Maybe we need to earn that title". It's the perfect opening line to what could easily have been a horribly bombastic portrait, a brilliantly humble, human response.

EA FOUNDED BY: TRIP HAWKINS

SOFTWARE ARTISTS: MIKE ABBOT, MATT ALEXANDER, DAN BUNTEN, JOHN FIELD, JON FREEMAN, DAVID MAYNARD, ANNE WESTFALL, BILL BUDGE

'IN SHORT, THEY ARE THE PEOPLE WHO MAY, OVER THE NEXT DECADE OR SO, CHANGE YOUR LIFE, AND FOR THAT REASON, YOU SHOULD KNOW THEM.'

ADVERT COPYRIGHT 1983 ELECTRONIC ARTS, SAN MATEO, CALIFORNIA

MANY PEOPLE MISTOOK THE COMPANY'S GEOMETRIC LOGO FOR READING 'EOA'.

▲ Above: 'Archon' cover art detail.

▶ Right: 'We See Farther' advertisement.

WE SEE FARTHER

ELECTRONIC ARTS™

HARD HAT MACK

ARCHON

M.U.L.E.

MURDER ON THE ZINDERNEUF

WORMS?

ELECTRONIC ARTS

Available for Apple, Atari, and Commodore computers.

Eureka!
1984

#INFO

RELEASED: 1984
PRIZE: £25,000
PRIZE DEADLINE: 31 DECEMBER 1985
WINNER: MATTHEW WOODLEY (AGE 15)
PRIZE PRESENTED BY: DOMINIC WHEATLEY AND MARK
STRACHAN AT THE PCW SHOW
NUMBER OF TIMES MATTHEW RANG THE ANSWERPHONE
BEFORE PLUCKING UP COURAGE TO LEAVE A MESSAGE
SAYING HE'D COMPLETED THE GAME: 3

Decades before Pokémon Go united strangers in the pursuit of mythical beasts apparently hiding in the streets around them, augmented reality stormed into bookshops. In 1979, a book was published in the UK that skilfully merged visual puzzles with the thrill of an actual treasure hunt. Kit Williams' Masquerade set the reader a series of puzzles that, when solved, revealed the real-world location in which a golden hare was hidden. It took almost three years for the treasure to be found.

Having already co-founded Games Workshop and co-authored the Fighting Fantasy book series, Ian Livingstone was starting to invest in videogames through the renowned company Domark. It took it's name from the fusion of the first names of the founders, Dominic Wheatley and Mark Straughan. Secondary trivia – Dominic Wheatley is the nephew of legendary occult novelist Dennis Wheatley. Livingstone saw the success of Masquerade, and with Domark's help, set about creating a similar challenge in a videogame.

Eureka was a text adventure, designed and written by Ian, that presented the player with a series of fiendish puzzles spanning five time periods. The last one, Modern

Caribbean, could only be unlocked once the first four had been completed. Upon solving the final puzzle, a telephone number was revealed. The first caller to dial in with the answer would receive a prize of £25,000.

The answer phone – which sat on the stairs at the home of Robert Bond, Domark's lawyer at the time – finally rang in 1985, and Matthew Woodley a teenager from the UK gave the correct answer and claimed the prize.

Prize-winning Matt went on to a career in videogames starting at Domark. Following the company mergers and acquisitions that ended

up transforming Domark into Eidos Interactive, he ended up working at Core Design in Derby. Ian Livingstone at the time was performing due diligence on the Eidos merger, and he noticed a new 3D adventure game that was being worked on at the Core studio. It was unusual to see a female protagonist in a videogame, and Ian thought it might be a commercial success...

▲ Above: Eureka! manual detail of Ian Livingstone.

▶ Right: Eureka! packaging, manual interior and game cassette.

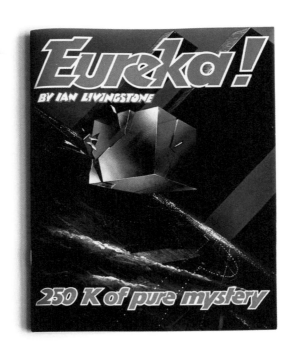

028.

EyeToy

2003

◆INFO

DESIGNED BY: RICHARD MARKS
MANUFACTURER: LOGITECH (KNOWN AS
LOGICOOL IN JAPAN)
RESOLUTION: 320 X 240 PIXELS
CONNECTION: USB 1.1
WEIGHT: 173 GRAMS
CABLE LENGTH: 2 METRES

Developed by Dr Richard Marks and Sony Computer Entertainment's London Studio, the EyeToy is a camera peripheral for the PlayStation 2 console. Released in 2003, the EyeToy resembled a computer webcam, but its primary purpose wasn't to allow video chatting. It was there to provide a new way of interacting with videogames. By using a combination of image analysis techniques and gestural input, the EyeToy effectively reinvented the videogame controller. Or to be more precise, it made you the controller. Rather than taking control of a virtual character, the EyeToy put you centre stage. You literally saw yourself on-screen superimposed onto the action. And rather than pressing buttons on a joypad to remotely controlling the action, you waved your arms around. And as well as showing you on the screen, the PlayStation and EyeToy recognized what you were doing.

If it was just used for waving your hand over 'next', 'back' and 'select' buttons in the interface before switching back to the Dual Shock 2 controller, that would be pretty cool. But imagine if you could swipe your arm at a ninja attacking you to deflect their blow. Or kick a football with your foot, or head it by well, heading

it. That wouldn't just be cool, it would be magical.

And that was precisely what EyeToy: Play did. EyeToy: Play was the first game to make use of the peripheral and was bundled with the camera when it was first released. A collection of minigames, EyeToy: Play has some standout experiences, such as the aforementioned Kung Fu and the altogether more unlikely Wishi Washi window cleaning simulation (possibly the first of its kind). Wishi Washi involved cleaning the suds and grime from a succession of virtual windows, all to the perhaps inevitable but nonetheless delightfully silly and appropriately British 'When I'm Cleaning Windows' by George Formby. The genius of Wishi Washi was the way that success ultimately revealed you on screen showing you not only how good you were but also reminding you just how extraordinary this hands-free gaming experience really was.

In truth, not all of EyeToy: Play's minigames were quite so successful, though each functioned as a tech demo showcasing a different aspect of the EyeToy system's functionality and potential. The potential was picked up by subsequent titles, with Sony releasing a number of titles specially

designed for EyeToy including sequels to EyeToy: Play as well as dancing games such as EyeToy: Groove and an exercise routine called EyeToy: Kinetic. As well as titles designed for the EyeToy, a number of other PlayStation 2 games included special modes or minigames that made use of the camera. Sony's SingStar and Konami's Dancing Stage series allowed players to see themselves singing and dancing on screen respectively, while Tony Hawk's Underground 2 was one of a number of games that let players scan their faces and map it to their character.

Having sold more than 10 million units in its lifetime, it came as no surprise that, with the release of the PlayStation 3, Sony announced a new camera peripheral. Rather ominously named the PlayStation Eye, this new device boasted a higher resolution than the original's 320x240 pixel capture and gave rise to new gaming experiences such as the Eye Pet virtual augmented reality creature simulation.

....

▼ Right (top): PlayStation 2 EyeToy Camera unit.

▶ Right (bottom): EyeToy: Play retail packaging and software.

Fallout 4 Pip-Boy Replica (and Stand)

2015

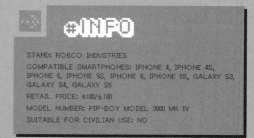

+INFO

STAND: ROBCO INDUSTRIES

COMPATIBLE SMARTPHONES: IPHONE 4, IPHONE 4S, IPHONE 5, IPHONE 5S, IPHONE 6, IPHONE 6S, GALAXY S3, GALAXY S4, GALAXY S5

RETAIL PRICE: $100/£100

MODEL NUMBER: PIP-BOY MODEL 3000 MK IV

SUITABLE FOR CIVILIAN USE: NO

For those not intimately familiar with the intricacies of Fallout 4's Pip-Boy, the device was manufactured by RobCo Industries before the War and issued to all Vault-Tec Vaults. Pip stands for 'Personal Information Processor' and, as this name suggests, the device's primary function is to store the user's personal statistics as well as give access to their inventory and maps. Also including a Geiger Counter (essential for post-nuclear operations), and a display that can be used as a torch in lowlight conditions, the Pip-Boy is worn on the wrist much like an oversized watch. It includes 64k of RAM, runs a bespoke Pip-OS operating system and is, of course, an entirely fictional item that was created for the Fallout game series and which doesn't actually exist in the real world.

Unless, that is, you purchased the special collector's edition of Bethesda's multi-award winning Fallout 4, in which case you will have received a Vault-Tec poster for keeping track of all your perks and, most importantly, a replica of the Pip-Boy itself (along with a RobCo Industries stand to ensure your Pip is displayed to its fullest advantage).

This special edition of the game was sold through only a handful of

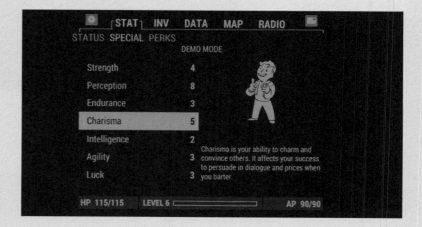

retailers, making it a much sought-after item, and one that added a new dimension to Fallout 4's game-play. But how could an ornament representing a piece of in-game tech add to the game-play? Well, the replica Pip-Boy isn't simply an ornament. For starters, it can actually be worn by the player. So, adjusting the foam cuff for maximum comfort, rotating the knobs, and bathing in the reflection of the flashing lights really makes you feel a part of the action. But that's not all. The Pip-Boy also includes a slot to slide in a smartphone. By running a companion app on the phone, the now complete Pip-Boy connects to the game and lets the

player manage their inventory, perks and holotapes – all from their wrist!

If that all sounds a little complicated, there's no need to panic, as the Fallout 4 Pip-Boy Edition also came with a Pip-Boy Pocket Guide to explain the device's operation. Given the amount of life-saving functionality in this piece of Pre-War wearable tech, the Pip-Boy Edition's £100 price starts to seem like a bargain (although please note that the smartphone is not included!)

▲ Above : Screenshot from companion smartphone app.

▲ Right: Fallout Pip-Boy Unit.

030.

Football Manager
(signed by Kevin Toms)

1982

#INFO

MEDIUM: CASSETTE

FEATURES INCLUDE: INJURY PROBLEMS, SAVE GAME FACILITY, MATCHES IN 3D GRAPHICS, YOU CAN EVEN BE SACKED

ADDICTIVE GAMES BASED IN: BOURNEMOUTH, UK

LOADING TIME: APPROXIMATELY 20 MINUTES

GAME PHASES: 1) OPTIONAL ACTIONS; 2) PLAYING A MATCH; 3) RESULTS OF MATCH; 4) WEEKLY BILLS; 5) TRANSFER MARKET

One of the deepest niches in videogames started here. Kevin Toms demonstrated just how amazing home computers in the early 1980s were by coding Football Manager entirely in BASIC*

Football Manager gave birth to an entire genre. It's important to remember that this wasn't a game about PLAYING football, like FIFA, Sensible Soccer and lots of other games that have followed – this was a game about simulating management. This was a game about training, transfers, finance, individual team statistics – it's not without reason that the game was mocked for being a 'playable spreadsheet'. Kevin Toms had created a simulation of work, and people loved it.

The goal of the game (yeah?) was to take your team from the fourth division and gradually make your journey to winning the first, perhaps taking some trophies home along the way. Even in its first release, the game offered the player a rich level of detail. Individual player statistics demanded your managerial attention. If a player was tired, they needed to be rested, their morale needed to be tended to, your squad needed to be assembled on a match by match basis to best beat the opposing team. Financial management played a part, too. Managers needed to negotiate transfers, take out bank loans to finance them... The mundane minutiae of the beautiful game was celebrated and the detail became a core part of what people loved about the experience.

Whilst lots of other areas of videogames were already rushing towards better and better graphics, Kevin Toms showed the world that an incredible amount of engagement and drama could be summoned up from simple text on a screen.

After the poorly received Football Manager 3, the series ended. It would be some time before Sports Interactive revived the brand name after their split from Eidos.

* BASIC. - Beginners All purpose Symbolic Instruction Code was a simple programming language designed to help anyone learn how to program a computer. Variations of it were built into lots of the early home computers.

....

◀ Right: Game-play screenshots.

▶ Far right: Football Manager retail packaging for Commodore 64 and ZX Spectrum (signed by creator Kevin Toms).

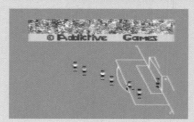

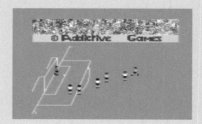

Freeloader

2002

•INFO

CREATED BY: DATEL
MADE IN: ENGLAND
ENDORSED, SPONSORED OR APPROVED BY NINTENDO: NO
'PLAY IMPORTED GAMES FROM ANY REGION ON ANY GAMECUBE
ADD LOADS OF NEW TITLES TO YOUR GAMECUBE COLLECTION INCLUDING GAMES THAT MAY NEVER BE RELEASED IN YOUR REGION
NO NEED TO MODIFY YOUR CONSOLE — KEEPS YOUR WARRANTY INTACT'

Because the videogames industry is so global in nature, with games being developed and distributed across the world, it is tempting to think that everybody everywhere has access to every game. This isn't true, and it never has been.

Some games don't get released in certain countries, or are heavily modified as they undergo translation or localization. If you've ever heard the phrase 'All your base are belong to us' and wondered where it came from or what it meant, well, that's a line from the European translation of the 1992 Mega Drive game Zero Wing, and you can bet it sounded better in the original Japanese.

Some games suffer audiovisual and game-play transformations as they make the jump from one country's TV standards to another. Take Sega's Sonic the Hedgehog, for example. Did you know that in Europe and Australasia, Sonic runs 17.5 per cent slower than he does in Japan or the US? PAL (Phase Alternate Line), the European and Australasian TV standard, specifies a different screen resolution and refresh rate than the NTSC (National Television Standards Council) standard used in Japan and the US. The same goes for The Legend of Zelda: A Link to the Past on the Super Nintendo Entertainment

System, Balloon Fight on the Nintendo Entertainment System... the list goes on and on.

And these are the games that do get released. What about the ones that never did? Like Animal Crossing. Wait, the original Animal Crossing was never released in Europe? That's right. Which is not to say that players in Europe didn't play it, just that there was never an official European release. But without an official release, what can you do? If you try to play a Japanese or US disc on a European GameCube, you just get an error message saying the disc isn't compatible. It's exactly the same as trying to play a DVD from one region on a player from another. So, you're stuck, right? Well, not quite. Enter the Freeloader.

Made in England by Datel, the Freeloader disc allowed games from any region to be played on any GameCube console. That meant that games like Animal Crossing that were never released in Europe could be played by European players willing to import a Japanese or American disc. With so many games never receiving a release outside Japan, for the real aficionado and collector, the Freeloader was an essential tool. The Freeloader worked by bypassing the checks that the console performed at

start-up, thereby stopping it rejecting discs not intended for play in that part of the world. It basically made the console region free.

Of course, in addition to the technical wizardry happening behind the scenes, the Freeloader relied on one other thing – importers. Because many videogames didn't receive a European release – and even when they were released, they were frequently subject to many months of delays after they'd come out elsewhere in the world, or were technically inferior, like Sonic – retailers specializing in import games were commonplace. Throughout the 1990s, either via adverts placed in magazines or independent stores, keen European gamers could source Japanese or US releases ahead of time that ran as intended.

Although this was all good news for consumers, videogame publishers weren't quite so keen, and sought to limit the 'grey import' market. With the connectivity of modern consoles, identifying modifications to hardware and software have become more automated and players now potentially run the risk of having their accounts suspended.

▶ Right: Datel Freeloader retail packaging with disc and instruction manual.

032.

Game & Watch: Ball

1980

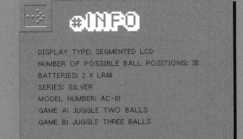

◆INFO

DISPLAY TYPE: SEGMENTED LCD
NUMBER OF POSSIBLE BALL POSITIONS: 30
BATTERIES: 2 X LR44
SERIES: SILVER
MODEL NUMBER: AC-01
GAME A: JUGGLE TWO BALLS
GAME B: JUGGLE THREE BALLS

Before the 3DS, before the DS, before even the venerable Game Boy, there was Nintendo's Game & Watch. There were 60 different games available in the Game & Watch series, which got its name because of Nintendo's ingenious combination of game-play and alarm clock functionality. They weren't wearable in any sense, and should really have been called 'Game & Clock', but that's not nearly as snappy.

It all started in 1980 with AC-01, or 'Ball' as it was more commonly known (or 'Toss Up' as it was originally named in North America). As neither of those names exactly suggest, the game-play is based around juggling. In 'Game A' two balls have to be caught and then tossed back into the air. In the more difficult 'Game B', an extra ball is added. Every ball caught nets 1 point in Game A, and a whopping ten points in Game B.

The player controls the on-screen juggler's arms, which can be in one of three positions. This precise manipulation is performed with the aid of just two buttons situated left and right of the screen which move the juggler's arms left and right.

This remarkable economy of interface, along with the provision of different Game A and B settings, are hallmarks of the Game & Watch series. So is the game structure and scoring system which, in the hands of

a skilled player, can theoretically continue ad infinitum (or until the two LR44 batteries run out).

So, where did the idea for the Game & Watch come from? Legend has it that inspiration struck Nintendo super-designer Gunpei Yokoi when he was travelling on the Shinkansen (aka the bullet train) and saw a businessman playing around with a pocket calculator. Legend doesn't record how he was playing with it, and whether or not he was just trying to write out rude words on the display – don't pretend you haven't. Heading back to Nintendo, Yokoi took the segmented display technology from the calculator, and combined it with some simple buttons for controlling the on-screen action (and that all-important alarm clock). So was born the Game & Watch.

Truth be told, Nintendo did make a number of actual wristwatches with built-in games in the 1990s, which probably better qualify to be called Game & Watch, but it was too late by then. The name will be forever associated with these LCD handheld systems.

Over time, new play styles and technologies were added to the line-up, with the Multi Screen series bringing two displays to games such as Donkey Kong and Green House, and multiplayer competition in the

Micro Vs. system games like Boxing (aka Punch Out in North America) and Donkey Kong 3.

In all, 59 Game & Watch titles were released for sale, but a special 60th title was available only to competition winners*. The Game & Watch has had quite an impressive legacy, with the directional pad going on to feature in most Nintendo console controllers, and the clamshell design of the Multi Screen series inspiring the Nintendo DS and 3DS handhelds.

As for Ball, a limited edition re-issue was made available to celebrate the 30th Anniversary of Game & Watch. For those not lucky enough to get their hands on this version, there was a DSiWare remake and you should definitely look out for Super Smash Bros., as Mr Game & Watch's throws look awfully familiar, almost as if he's juggling his opponents...

* The 60th Game & Watch game was given to winners of Nintendo's Formula 1 Grand Prix Competition. Housed in a yellow box in the shape of the character Nintendo used to advertise their Famicom Disk System, it is a yellow-cased version of Game & Watch Super Mario Bros. Only 10,000 were ever made.

▶ Right: Nintendo Game & Watch: Ball, unit and packaging.

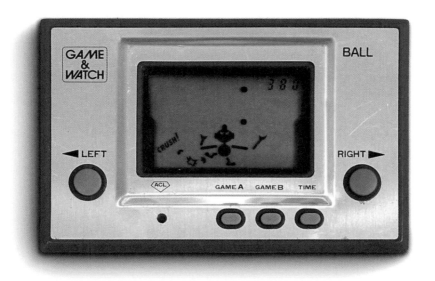

Game Child
MK II

1993

INFO

INSPIRED BY: NINTENDO GAME BOY
POWER: 1 X AA BATTERY
MKII GAMES: FOOTBALL, SPACE WAR, DESERT WAR
SOUND FUNCTIONS: ON/OFF
PAUSE FUNCTIONS: ON/OFF
CARTRIDGE SLOT: NO
IN 2013, THE FILM 'ASHENS AND THE QUEST FOR THE GAME CHILD'
FOLLOWED THE UK COMEDIAN'S SEARCH FOR THE CONSOLE.

The Game Child is a handheld game console heavily inspired by the Nintendo Game Boy. It probably goes without saying that despite some cosmetic similarities – and a somewhat more inclusive name than the system its look is based on – this is not an official Nintendo product. It isn't a clone of the Game Boy either. In fact, appearances aside, it has very little in common with the best-selling handheld platform.

The Game Child's display actually has far more in common with Nintendo's earlier Game & Watch series, using a segmented LCD rather than a pixelated display. Like a calculator, each of the various elements are either 'lit' or 'unlit', rather than being drawn from individual pixels.

But this is far from the end of the differences between Boy and Child. Where Nintendo's system had removable cartridges that allowed players to load new games, the Game Child's 'cartridge slot' is where the batteries go. It cannot accept cartridges, and ships with just one game hard coded into the system.

This is odd, seeing as the back of the Game Child box shows screen shots for multiple games. For the original Game Child, there's Football, Space War and Desert War. Looking carefully at the original Game Child, a question arises. Each game has different graphics – even if the

actual gameplay does share marked similarities – but with no cartridge slot and no other obvious way of switching between games on the unit, how could this work? Given that the Game Child is already sailing close to the wind in terms of its resemblance to the Game Boy, is this multiple game claim simply a case of overenthusiastic advertising? Well, not quite.

The original Game Child is a single-game system, but there really are three different games – because there are three different Game Childs (Game Children?) For the first generation, Football, Space War, and Desert War are available. So, these Children are actually Triplets. They're not identical, but they are very hard to tell apart. Each is delivered in an identical box adorned with screenshots of all three games. From the outside, each version is distinguishable only by the sticker on the box carefully stuck near(ish) the appropriate screenshot.

So, what do you do if you want to play all the games in the Game Child library? Well, that means you Gotta Catch 'Em All. No wait, that's the Game Boy. Sorry Children.

The Game Child MK II switches things up a little though. Upgraded, enhanced, and perhaps just a little more mature. The brightly coloured bezel around the display is the most obvious difference and holds the key to one of the greatest

changes. The MK II truly is a multi-game, offering no fewer than 6 games in 1! But don't waste any valuable playing time searching for a cartridge slot round the back because you still won't find one. It's actually those coloured bezels that are removable. The whole piece, complete with the name of the game printed on, lifts right out. Funny how that idea never caught on, or perhaps the Game Child MK II is just ahead of its time.

◄ Right (top): Game Child MK II.

▶ Right (bottom) and Above: Retail packaging front and rear showing game screens.

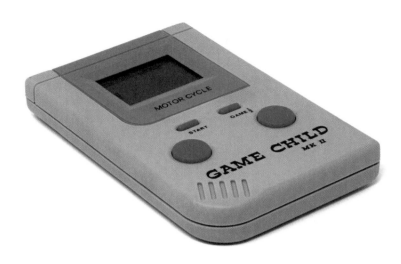

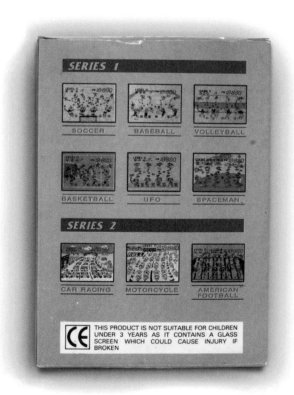

034.

Game Genie

1990

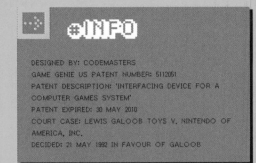

#INFO

DESIGNED BY: CODEMASTERS
GAME GENIE US PATENT NUMBER: 5112051
PATENT DESCRIPTION: 'INTERFACING DEVICE FOR A
COMPUTER GAMES SYSTEM'
PATENT EXPIRED: 30 MAY 2010
COURT CASE: LEWIS GALOOB TOYS V. NINTENDO OF
AMERICA, INC.
DECIDED: 21 MAY 1992 IN FAVOUR OF GALOOB

According to the packaging and the label on the front of the device, the Game Genie is a 'video game enhancer'. Not sure exactly what a 'videogame enhancer' is? Well, perhaps another way to phrase it would be that the Game Genie is a videogame cheating system. That's what everybody that owned the Game Genie actually called it. Not that Codemasters, the UK developer that created the device, would ever have used the word 'cheat' of course.

Cheating in videogames is a tricky and evocative subject, especially when dealing with multiplayer and online gaming. But that's not what we're talking about here. The Game Genie isn't about aimbots that automatically aim weapons or wallhacks that let them see through normally solid objects – and that get people banned from playing online if they get caught. No, it's not that sort of cheating. It's cheating in the sense of 'cheat code', which was a phrase common in the 1980s and 1990s and referred to some modification of the game's operation to alter its operation in some way. Magazines would routinely run sections publishing cheat codes that activated certain features hidden in games by their programmers. Before that, in the era of 8-bit computers like the Commodore 64, lists of 'POKEs' that could by typed in prior to running a game were commonplace. 'POKE' statements allowed players to access and modify certain memory addresses to influence the game's behaviour.

The Game Genie operated in a not dissimilar way by temporarily modifying the game's code. The original Game Genie device was created for the Nintendo Entertainment System and released in 1990. It shipped with a 'codebook' that contained multiple codes for most of the popular games of the time. Distributed in America by Camerica and Galoob, the Game Genie incurred the wrath of Nintendo, who considered an infringement of copyright. The courts saw otherwise and, after a brief period where it was unavailable in the US, the Game Genie went back on sale. And sell it most certainly did. Five million units of the original Game Genie products were sold worldwide.

So what were these 'cheats' then? Many of them involved giving the player extra lives, or even infinite lives to tackle their games. Some gave invincibility or access to more powerful weapons or armour. But plenty of cheats weren't focused on making the game easier to play or giving the player an unfair advantage. Sometimes, it was just about having fun with the game by glitching

graphics and sound or getting access to areas that were supposed to be out of bounds or even graphics and items that were unused in the final game but looking in the depths of the code. So that's not really cheating in the way we understand it today. Perhaps that's why Codemasters preferred to call the Game Genie an 'enhancer'.

In fact, so popular are the enhancements that many classic videogame console emulators include support for Game Genie codes.

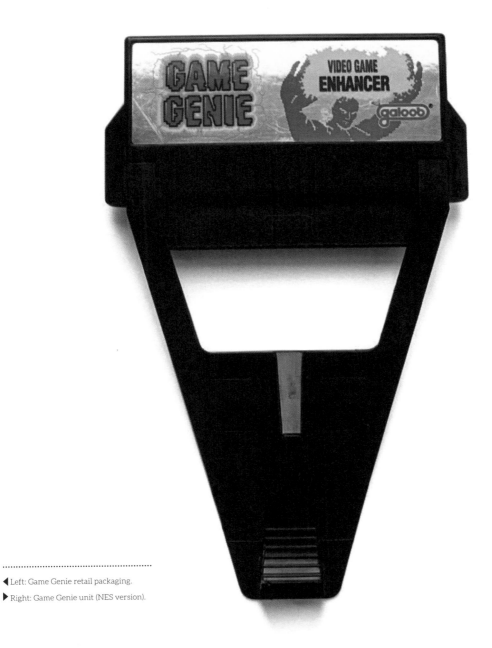

◀ Left: Game Genie retail packaging.
▶ Right: Game Genie unit (NES version).

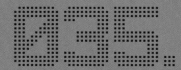

035.

GAME
Trade-In bag

2012

RETAILER: GAME (UK)
THE SMALL PRINT: TRADE-INS MUST BE COMPLETE,
IN WORKING ORDER AND OF SATISFACTORY QUALITY.
IMPORTED GAMES ARE EXCLUDED FROM TRADE-IN...
TRADE-IN PRICES ARE SUBJECT TO THE INSPECTION
OF THE COMPLETE PRODUCT. TRADE-IN OFFERS ARE
OPEN TO MEMBERS OF THE PUBLIC ONCE AND GAME
RESERVES THE RIGHT TO REFUSE ANY OFFER TO
ANYONE BELIEVED TO BE REPRESENTING A TRADE BUYER.

What do you do with your old videogames? Do you neatly package them up, making sure all the instruction manuals and warranty cards are together, and put everything on a shelf in alphabetical order? Or do you just throw them roughly into the back of a cupboard somewhere, and forget all about them until you're forced to tidy the house? Do you hand them on to a friend or family member? Put them in a yard sale? Donate them to a charity shop? Perhaps, like a growing number of people, you trade them in and use the money you receive to help purchase the next game.

The trade-in market, or 'second sale' market as it's sometimes called, has become a significant part of the videogame economy. It's a controversial one, too. For players, the potential benefits are clear. You get to play the game and then recoup some of the monetary value in order to buy the next game. Exactly how much money you get depends on a few factors, including the condition it's in (you did keep all those instruction books and warranty cards?), how rare the game is, and how popular it still is.

For videogame developers and publishers, the second sale market doesn't work so well. The problem is that they don't see the money on these trade-in transactions. When a game is sold first time round, some of the money goes to the retailer, some to the distributor, and some to the publisher and developer. But, when a retailer sells a game that has been traded in, they keep all the money on that transaction. Consider that one copy of the game might be bought, traded-in, re-bought, re-traded-in, re-re-bought and re-re-traded in, and you see the problem for the publisher. But for retailers, it's great – pure profit – which is why they're so keen to promote the market.

So keen, in fact, that in the late 2000s, UK retailer GAME placed bags in their stores that customers could take away and fill with their unwanted games and consoles to bring back and exchange for new games and consoles. The message was clear: new games are better than old games.

Even though you might not have seen one of these GAME Trade-in bags before, they do look familiar, don't they? They do have an unnerving resemblance to the kinds of things you might see balanced on somebody's lap on a particularly turbulent transatlantic flight. And they do, perhaps, have the effect of marking out your old games and consoles as digital vomit.

If nothing else, the bag helps us answer one age-old question that's been causing arguments for decades. What's the best game? That's easy, the best game is always the next game.

3 easy steps to great savings.

1. Fill this bag with your used games.

2. Bring them in to any **GAME** store.

3. Get cash or credit to spend whenever you like.

For more information go to
game.co.uk/tradein

GAME
START HERE

▲ Above: Rear view showing instructions and terms and conditions.

▶ Right: GAME Trade-In bag (front).

036.

Goldeneye 007

1997

As any videogame fan will tell you, movie tie-ins are almost always terrible – lazy, derivative game designs intended to cash in on the popularity of an existing franchise. And as any PC-gaming fan will tell you, First Person Shooters only work on PCs and not on consoles. You need a mouse and keyboard, and a joypad just won't cut it.

At least, that's what they thought in 1996. By the time Goldeneye 007 was released for the Nintendo 64 in 1997, things were a little different. Here was a truly original game that both drew on and developed its movie license (to kill) and which not only (death-) matched PC FPS gaming, but bettered it by making you forget all about mice, keyboards and WSAD controls. Oh, and there was the small matter of that four-player split screen mode as well. It's hardly surprising that Goldeneye 007 went on to outsell Super Mario 64, Super Mario Kart 64 and The Legend of Zelda: Ocarina of Time in the US, and has subsequently been voted one of the best games of all time.

What is slightly more surprising is that 8 of the 10-strong development team were new to videogame development. And that the game was originally intended to be an on-rails shooter, in the style of Sega's Virtua Cop. And that the multiplayer modes

were added to the game at the very last minute almost as an afterthought.

In fact, it's the fluidity and lack of a dogmatic design plan to which the developers partly attribute the success of the game's eventual design. Features could be added if they were deemed to advance the game-play and they were added by the development team rather than at the insistence of a publisher or marketing executive removed from the process of actual development. Moreover, Rare's owners allowed the team to take their time over the development rather than rushing to hit the release of the film.

This combination of time, enthusiasm and flexibility explains why Goldeneye 007 brims over with innovations like dual-wielded weapons, years before they came to the Halo series. It's also why the doorways are so narrow (because they're modelled on real doorways rather than the cavernous apertures more common in FPS games that let you effortlessly glide through them). It's why the player can see through windows but enemies can't (meaning that you can sneak around and take careful aim) and why your weapon makes a noise that alerts enemies (so rather than going in all guns blazing, you can be economical and play what turns out to be one of the first stealth action games).

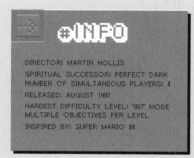

#INFO

DIRECTOR: MARTIN HOLLIS
SPIRITUAL SUCCESSOR: PERFECT DARK
NUMBER OF SIMULTANEOUS PLAYERS: 4
RELEASED: AUGUST 1997
HARDEST DIFFICULTY LEVEL: '007' MODE
MULTIPLE OBJECTIVES PER LEVEL
INSPIRED BY: SUPER MARIO 64

Of course, this is not to say that every one of the team's suggestions made its way into the final game. Having the player reload their weapon by pulling out and reconnecting the vibrating Rumble Pak from the bottom of the N64's controller was just one idea that ended up on the cutting room floor.

One additional feature that was not exactly left out but was disabled and subsequently found and reactivated by fans and hackers is a fully-functional ZX Spectrum emulator built right into the game. Find out how to activate it, and you can play 10 of the games Rare developed for the iconic 1980s Sinclair home computer.

▼ Right: Goldeneye 007 packaging, game cartridge and 'golden' controller.

037

Goldeneye 007
design documents

#INFO

DIRECTOR: MARTIN HOLLIS
SPIRITUAL SUCCESSOR: PERFECT DARK
NUMBER OF SIMULTANEOUS PLAYERS: 4
RELEASED: AUGUST 1997
HARDEST DIFFICULTY LEVEL: '007' MODE
MULTIPLE OBJECTIVES PER LEVEL INSPIRED BY: SUPER
MARIO 64

Goldeneye 007, one of the most acclaimed videogames of all time, had a remarkably analogue, paper-based origin. Karl Hilton, art director of an incredibly small team at Rare, was tasked with creating the visual world for Bond to play in.

Working from the design blueprints provided by the film production team, he started out by sketching basic 2D versions of the environments they knew they wanted to include. Following that, the team spent at lot of time at Leavesden studios in the UK visiting the set of the movie. Karl shot hundreds of reference photographs of the sets, many of which formed the basis of the textures used in the game. You can see some of those here.

Of course, one of the things about movie sets is that they're usually lacking the 'fourth wall' of a scene, in order to accommodate the camera and crew. If you're making a videogame however, you can't get away with three walls. When the player spins around they need to see something! Karl spent a lot of time imagining the 'missing' parts of the Goldeneye set in order to create a truly immersive world for the player. The sets themselves were far too small to create an interesting enough space, so

he set about expanding the world the filmmakers had built. This itself though, was hindered by the limited processing power of the Nintendo 64.

In these relatively early days of 3D, the console was unable to draw long distances ahead of the player so the team needed to design their way around these constraints. Karl created gateways and 'dog leg' corridors, occluding the view of the player and managing those short draw-distances!

Once the basic outline had been created, David Doak would play through basic 'blocked out' versions of a level, feeding back where props and other elements like spawn-points

should be added. You can see those elements on the map, the beginnings of the rapid iterations of the levels.

Collaborative, on-paper game design was an essential part of the design process for Goldeneye and many other similar games from that period. It's a process that's been all but replaced now by the rapid prototyping afforded by the technology of modern 3D game engines.

▲ Above: Reference photographs from the *Goldeneye* movie set, taken by Karl Hilton.

▶ Right: Maps for Goldeneye 007 levels drawn by Karl Hilton.

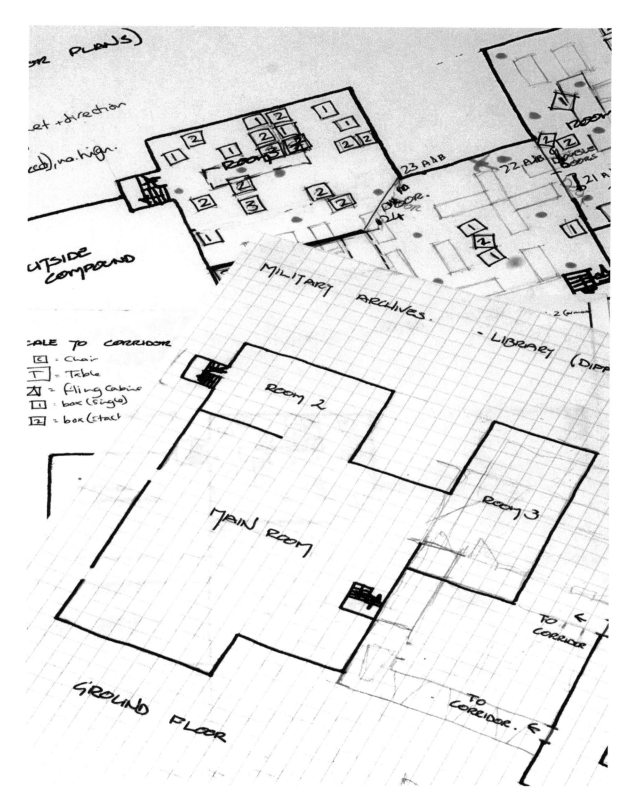

...R PLANS)

...t + direction

...ed) no. high.

OUTSIDE
COMPOUND

Room 3

23 AAB

No
DOOR.
424

22 AAB   DOUBLE
          DOORS

21 A

ROOM

2 (cor...

MILITARY ARCHIVES.

- LIBRARY (DIFF

...CALE TO CORRIDOR
☐ C = Chair
☐ T = Table
☐ = Filing Cabinet
☐ 1 = box (single)
☐ 2 = box (stack)

ROOM 2

ROOM 3

MAIN ROOM

TO
CORRIDOR

TO
CORRIDOR.

GROUND
FLOOR

(The) Golf Construction Set

1985

As much as players love to play, they love to create. 'User-generated content' became a buzz-phrase in the mid-2000s. The success of Media Molecule's 'LittleBigPlanet' and the apparently unstoppable ubiquity of Mojang's 'Minecraft' led gamers towards a much more expressive experience than they had been used to before. Games weren't fixed anymore, rather they were open tools offered to players to create, share and play within. The apparently limitless freedom within something like Minecraft was arrived at through a long lineage of player creativity.

The PC game community began modifying games (modding, as it was known) in earnest with the release of DOOM. This first-person shooter was hugely important for many reasons, but its open invitation for players to remake the maps within it was the most remarkable. Helpfully coinciding with a usable internet, it ushered in a new age of creativity. As players created new maps they could play within DOOM itself and swapped them over the fledgling internet, a new generation of level designers were training.

It's important to remember that level editors and game creation tools for the mainstream consumer existed

long before then. Bill Budge's seminal 'Pinball Construction Set' was one of the most well-known. An early title from a fledgling Electronic Arts (and featured in their noted 'we see farther' campaign) it offered players the chance to create their own playable pinball tables as independent pieces of software, swapping them without the need for the original game. Whilst it wasn't the first, Budge's game set the template for many that followed.

The Shoot-'em-up Construction Kit, created by Sensible Software in 1987 was particularly notable. This package, created by the team behind Sensible Soccer and Cannon Fodder, allowed users to create their own self-contained games which could be freely distributed. Golf Construction Set, released by Ariolasoft in 1985, was one of the more marginal.

#INFO

COURSES: FOUR (WENTWORTH OLD COURSE, THE BELFRY, SUNNINGDALE, ROYAL ST GEORGES)

GAME CONCEPT: DAVID BISHOP AND CHRIS PALMER

LIMITED EDITION INCLUDED FREE 'STROKESAVER OFFICIAL WENTWORTH COURSE GUIDE'

ZZAP!64 MAGAZINE REVIEW SCORE (JULY 1986): 79%

ZZAP!64 OVERALL COMMENT: 'AN INTERESTING ATTEMPT THAT DOESN'T QUITE HIT THE MARK BECAUSE OF SOME SILLY LITTLE FAULTS, BUT PROBABLY WORTH FORKING OUT FOR IF YOU'RE A GOLFING TYPE.'

▲ Above: (The) Golf Construction Set cassette software (save protection removed on blue cassette).

▶ Right: (The) Golf Construction Set manual.

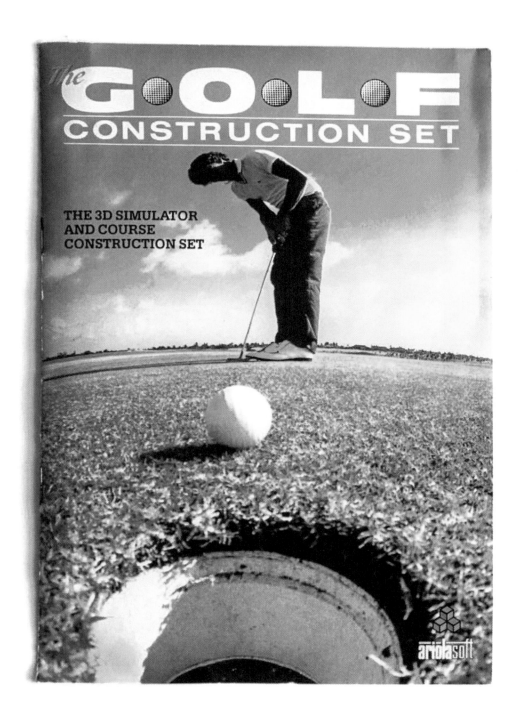

The # G·O·L·F
CONSTRUCTION SET

**THE 3D SIMULATOR
AND COURSE
CONSTRUCTION SET**

ariolasoft

Guitar Hero On Tour Guitar Grip

2008

Throughout the 2000s, music games were big. Who didn't secretly harbour dreams of rocking out on stage, striking poses with a Fender Strat or laying down a 20-minute virtuoso drum solo? While Shea Stadium might have been a little way off for some, the Guitar Hero and Rock Band series were a pretty good substitute. Guitar-shaped controllers let players strum along as rhythm guitarists, prop up the low end as bassists, or shred their way through lead lines. Advanced performance techniques let players do dive bombs with the whammy bar as well as hammer-ons and pull-offs.

Specially-mixed tracks let players jam along with their favourite recordings, and there was serious talk in the music press about whether the popularity of these games would cause a new generation to take up learning the instruments for real. Could we see a wave of new musicians inspired by videogames? Could it be that videogames might even help would-be players learn the guitar or drums for real?

We might still be waiting for news that the next Hendrix cut their teeth on a game controller, but the popularity of these games was such that artists were keen to have their music featured. Special Editions of Guitar Hero included Aerosmith, Van Halen and Metallica, while The Beatles Rock Band set included mini replicas of Paul's Hofner bass, Ringo's Ludwig drum kit, John's Rickenbacker 325 and the Gibson Duo Jet that George would have played in the band's early days. Just in case the scale of the music game's significance still isn't clear, this was the first time The Beatles' catalogue of recordings was made available in digital form. Before iTunes, before Spotify, there was The Beatles Rock Band.

Of course, every would-be band member also harbours dreams of going on tour and, while the Guitar Hero guitars are eminently portable, having to lug around a game console, TV set and all the cables starts to feel like you need to employ a road crew. That part of the simulation could be getting a bit too realistic.

But we have portable gaming consoles, so why not create a version of Guitar Hero that you can take on the road? Enter the fanatically named, and almost as fanatically fiddly and complex, Guitar Hero: On Tour.

There's a lot to like about Guitar Hero: On Tour, not least because there is a lot to Guitar Hero: On Tour. First up, there's a customized DS complete with Guitar Hero logo. Then there's the game. Nothing unbelievably out of the ordinary so far. And then there's the

◆INFO

DEVELOPER: VICARIOUS VISIONS
PACK INCLUDES: GUITAR HERO: ON TOUR
GAME; GUITAR GRIP, ADJUSTABLE STRAP,
PICK STYLUS
NUMBER OF FRET BUTTONS ON
GUITAR GRIP: 4
STRUMMING: USING TOUCHSCREEN AND
GUITAR PICK STYLUS
ARTISTS INCLUDE: RED HOT CHILI
PEPPERS, OK GO, THE DOOBIE BROTHERS
AND STRAY CATS

controller which is, most definitely, out of the ordinary. Even by the audacious standards set by Guitar Hero, this is pretty out there. The buttons that would ordinarily be mounted on the neck of the guitar are set into a cross between a bracket and a knuckle duster that straps around the back of the hand. Using the fingers of one hand to tap the buttons, the other grasps the plectrum – yes that right, the plectrum – and strums the DS display. It's as ingenious as it is unlikely, and as incredible as it is brilliant.

For those who are about to rock – by strumming a touchscreen and pressing coloured buttons in the palm of your hand – we salute you!

▶ Right: 'Guitar Grip' controller, 'Pick' stylus and DS console with custom sticker.

Haze
Mints

2006

When journalists are dispatched to trade shows they often play a game with each other to see who can acquire the most interesting 'swag'. Promotional items emblazoned with the graphics of the game or studio they're promoting can range from useful and tasteful to disposable and bad. For every heavy-thread Nintendo tee-shirt, there's a terrible antithesis. Whilst many of these items are consigned to the refuse within a few months, some of them acquire more meaning as the years pass and the circumstances around the brand they're promoting change.

Free Radical Design were one of the most celebrated developers of the early 2000s. Formed by members of the original Goldeneye 64 team after leaving Rare, their 'Timesplitters' series on Playstation 2 became one of the defining IPs of the platform.

At E3 in 2006, they presented a preview of a new first-person-shooter title, Haze. This was an ambitious departure in style for the company, leaving behind their early cartoon-like graphics and experimenting with an adult, narrative format. Haze was a complex story about ethics, privatization of the military and the morally ambiguous choices given to the player. Their presentation at E3 was reflective of this new direction. A scientist, representing the shady

'Mantle' corporation from the game, ushered journalists into a briefing room where he went about introducing them to their new, performance-enhancing drug, 'nectar'. As the presentation wore on, problems with the drug were gradually revealed before the show was terminated by a military general, annoyed at the disclosure of problems with the drug. As he quickly ushered journalists out of the door, he pressed a packet of this candy into their palm.

Sadly, Haze was poorly received on release. Further brutal treatment at the hands of publishers forced Free Radical into administration in 2009.

▣INFO

GAME CREATED IN: NOTTINGHAM, UK
MINT CREATED IN: CANADA
GAME RELEASED IN: 2008
GAME METACRITIC SCORE: 55
MINT CALORIFIC VALUE: 1

▲ Above: Haze game-play screenshot.

▶ Right: Haze promotional mints packaging front and rear.

Nutrition Facts
Serving Size 2 Pieces (0.2 g)
Servings per container about 41
Calories 1

Not a significant source of other nutrients.
*Percent Daily Value (%DV) are based on a 2,000 calorie diet.

Amount/Serving	%DV*
Total Fat 0g	0%
Sodium 0mg	0%
Total Carbohydrate 0g	1%
Sorbitol 0g	
Protein 0g	

INGREDIENTS: Sorbitol, Guarana Seed Extract (22% Caffeine), Xylitol, Peppermint Oil, Crystal Menthol Magnesium Sterate, Sucralose, Vitamin B12

7159-E6 05/2008

PACKAGE MADE IN CHINA
MINT MADE IN CANADA
DISTRIBUTED BY
JOCO BRANDS
CORONA DEL MAR, CA 92625
WWW.VOJOENERGY.COM

8 53797 00004

041.

Jakks Pacific 'Plug It In And Play' Atari TV Games

2003

◉INFO

POWER: 9V BATTERY
AV CONNECTION: COMPOSITE VIDEO AND
MONAURAL AUDIO ON PHONE JACKS
BUILT-IN GAMES INCLUDE: SPACE INVADERS,
PONG, YAR'S REVENGE
MADE IN: CHINA
COPYRIGHT: 2002 JAKKS PACIFIC, INC,
MALIBU, CALIFORNIA 90265
CONTROLS: JOYSTICK, FIREBUTTON, SELECT,
START, RESET, ON/OFF SWITCH

The explosion in the popularity of retro-gaming over the past decade or so has given players keen to seek out classic gaming experiences a wide variety of options to choose from. There are snippets of old games included in new ones, such as Namco's PlayStation Ridge Racer conversion, which treats the player to a few rounds of Galaxian before the racing begins. There are playable versions of Space Harrier and Hang On in Shenmue's You Arcade, and collectible NES games within Animal Crossing. And then there are collections packaged by developers and publishers, such as Sega's Ultimate Mega Drive/Genesis Collections and the Namco Museum series. For those wishing to look beyond officially sanctioned collections, there are emulators and ROMs aplenty that give access to games on countless computer, console and handheld systems.

While the ability to emulate older systems is technically impressive, there's still something missing. It's not just the absence of that 1990s context which you could probably recreate with a dash of Grunge or Britpop depending on your taste. What's missing is the tactility of the original controllers. Playing Mega Drive Sonic the Hedgehog is only partly about the look and sound of Green Hill Zone. The feel of the Mega Drive joypad's

buttons and D-Pad is an important part of the experience. Being able to roll your thumb across the top of the NES pads A and B buttons to run and jump in Super Mario Bros. doesn't just reactivate nostalgic feelings but also allows 30 years of muscle memory to kick in.

The US toy manufacturer recognized this when it licensed a selection of games from Atari's 2600 back catalogue. Rather than package the games with a generic joypad controller, these recreations of Asteroids, Pong and Breakout are played with something that looked and, importantly, felt like an Atari 2600 joystick. That characteristic stuffiness to the stick that sometimes feels so unresponsive you worry that you might break it by pushing too hard, that's the feeling of 2600 gaming.

And it wasn't just that Jakks Pacific shipped their 2600 collection with an Atari joystick. They shipped the games in an Atari joystick. No separate console to plug them into. The joystick was the console and controller all in one. Two cables protruding from the back supplied mono audio and a composite video signal, giving a characteristic (if not wholly authentic) blurriness and noisiness to the audiovisual output while maintaining a level of compatibility with modern

television that the original consoles could not rival.

However, before we proclaim this as the ultimate Atari 2600 for the modern age, there are a few caveats. Firstly, the Plug-It-In-And-Play Atari joystick ships with just 10 games. While this represents a good selection, it omits far more than it includes. So, what we have is: Adventure, Asteroids, Breakout, Centipede, Circus Atari, Gravitar, Missile Command, Pong, Volleyball, and Yars' Revenge. But there is no E.T. The Extra Terrestrial, no Pac-Man (the original system's bestselling game) and no Space Invaders. Additionally, these are not emulations but ports of the original games. This means that while the controller itself has an impressive degree of authenticity, graphics and sound of the included games are subtly (and sometimes not so subtly) different from their forebears. Ironically, many of these embedded gaming systems are based on a so-called Nintendo-on-a-Chip system, which means that Atari 2600 games are written on an emulation of NES hardware. It may not be authentic, but it's certainly fascinating.

▶ Right: Jakks Pacific Atari 'Plug It In And Play' unit.

042.

Jet Set Willy
Software Protection Card

1984

Piracy didn't used to be something you downloaded. Napster and all its descendants have led us into a modern world where copyright offenses are almost surreally easy to commit. Back in the day, it was much harder to steal someone's intellectual property. Pirates these days...

With the advent of hi-fi in the home came the first instances of a new kind of technology, the tape-to-tape recorder. One unit, with two tape decks allowed one to make a copy of the other. Suddenly, duplication was domesticated. The music industry was the first to be hit. Whilst today we might remember them fondly as 'mix-tapes', collections of songs from different albums put together on a blank tape for a friend, back then they were known in the music industry as 'Killing Music'. The pirate cassette is covered elsewhere in this book, however. This entry is about one of the most famous efforts to stop it.

'Jet Set Willy', the sequel to the wildly successful 'Manic Miner', was released in 1984 by Liverpool-based publisher Software Projects. Coded by one man, the enigmatic Matthew Smith, it was predicted to be a commercial smash-hit follow-up and Software Projects wanted to do all it

could to protect its revenue.

The mechanism for doing this was an ingenious, if delicate system, that relied on the use of a small 'copy protection card' which came packaged with the game. On the card was a grid, in each cell an apparently random set of four colours. As soon as the game loaded, the user was asked to enter the code at a given grid location, the code dictated by the order of the colours. If the code is entered correctly, the game starts. Get it wrong twice and the computer is restarted, demanding that the player spends another five minutes reloading the game.

The assumption on the part of Software Projects' was of course that no-one would be bothered to actually copy out the grid codes and reproduce them. This assumption was rapidly proved wrong by the schoolchildren of the UK, whose dedication to piracy was unmatched.

Perhaps more remarkably, a mainstream videogame magazine of the time published a readers' letter which explained a way of 'getting round the problem' using a quick programming hack before loading. In the early eighties, hobbyist culture could confront copy protection as part of daily invention. The

NUMBER OF COLOURS PER SQUARE: 4
(RED, GREEN, BLUE, YELLOW)
PATENT: PENDING
IN JUNE 1984, THE UK MAGAZINE 'YOUR COMPUTER' (VOL. 4 NO. 6) PRINTED THE FOLLOWING CODE FOR CIRCUMVENTING JET SET WILLY'S COPY PROTECTION
SYSTEM: 25 POKE 23672,0;POKE 23673,0;POKE 23674,0
ORIGINAL PRICE OF JET SET WILLY: £5.95
PRICE OF JUNE 1984 ISSUE OF 'YOUR COMPUTER': 85P

videogame itself was something to be manipulated, as the same letter included a hack to add an infinite number of lives to the game.

▲ Above: Jet Set Willy cassette software

▶ Right: Jet Set Willy cassette packaging and software protection card

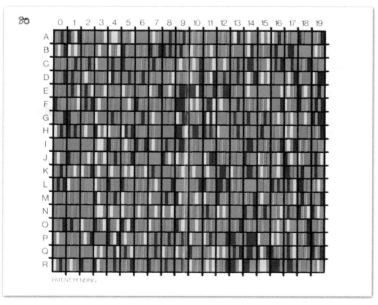

043.

KP Skips Action Biker with Clumsy Colin

1985

The early 80s were an especially fertile time for gaming. Small teams and individual developers would produce prolific amounts of work, some of which just modified existing games, some of which was breathtakingly experimental. The velocity of the games business attracted lots of people, creatively and commercially...

Alison Beasley, who is now a veteran of the PR side of the games industry, recalled starting to work for a small company called Mastertronic in 1984.

"I'd just moved up from Somerset to the West End to work in this amazingly fast-moving office. It was on Park Road, opposite Regents Park, the Darlings twins (who would go on to form Codemasters) rented a flat three floors above the office."

Mastertronic bought about a revolution in the UK games industry. Embracing the momentum with which new games were being created, they embraced the opportunity. Their first move was to create 'pocket money' games. Priced at £1.99, they were well within reach of everyone, and at that price, why not take a chance? Hundreds of thousands of people did.

This was helped by their other big innovation, in games retail. At the time, computer software was still a marginal pursuit. Largely the province of hobbyist shops and specialist enthusiast stores which were not always the most inviting place for potential non-gamers, Mastertronic changed all that. Alison remembers, "We sold them anywhere

that would take them. Newsagents, garages, corner shops but also high street nationals like Boots and Toys R Us – we put games out into the wild and people loved it. Our players were incredibly loyal. "

With so many new games, publishers started to look to other media for inspiration. Whilst Hollywood movies, TV shows and pop music provided a rich seam of brands to shape into games, Mastertronic looked elsewhere. To the grocery store...

Alison remembers,"Clumsy Colin, was one of the first brand-linked games to be made in the UK. There had been a few film, sports and arcade licenses but this was one of the first to be product linked.

"I think it came about from one of the Mastertronic bosses, Martin Alper, noticing that the KP brand had created a character for one of their Snacks, Clumsy Colin, and then matching that with a motorbike game that Mr Chips, one of our favourite developers, was working on."

KP Skips are prawn-cocktail flavoured snacks, similar to Chinese prawn crackers.

"Back then of course, the association with games was really positive. These were computer games, not arcade games. They were in peoples' lounges, they were family things, so it was a really positive thing for everyone.

"Clumsy Colin performed well, but I don't think they pursued many more licenses. Mastertronic released a lot of games every week, margins were tight and they could sell without paying for licenses."

#INFO

ALSO KNOWN AS: KP SKIPS ACTION
BIKER WITH CLUMSY COLIN (UK)

PUBLISHER: MASTERTRONIC

PROMOTIONAL TIE-IN WITH: KP SKIPS
PRAWN COCKTAIL TAPIOCA/POTATO
SNACKS

SKIPS FIRST LAUNCHED IN: 1974

THE GAME-PLAY, GRAPHICS AND PLOT OF
THE COMMODORE 64 AND ZX SPECTRUM
VERSIONS OF THE GAME ARE QUITE
DIFFERENT.

COMMODORE 64 SOUNDTRACK COMPOSED
BY: ROB HUBBARD

▲ Above: Game-play screenshot
(Commodore 64 version).

▶ Right: Commodore 64 version
cassette and retail packaging.

Mastertronic will be remembered as a publisher that launched the careers of many leaders of the games industry. Perhaps more than any publisher, they put games into the hands of the people. Hands that stank of prawn-cocktail.

044.
Larazade
2001

Whilst the star of Lara Croft might not burn quite as bright as it did when she first burst onto the celebrity scene, there are few that have ever had as big an impact. As time passes, it's easy to forget just how big Lara was in the 1990s. The original 'it' girl.

Let's briefly set the scene... A new government had swept into Britain with a younger Prime Minister at the helm, Britpop was storming the music scene, 'Cool Britannia' was in full flow exporting arts and culture globally, the Spice Girls were promoting 'girl-power' alongside their latest single –there was a white heat around the cultural life of the country for a while. Into the middle of this, PlayStation had been launched. Sony had given homes a different kind of games machine and marketed it in a wholly different, smarter way. With its four symbols branding its iconography across infinite locations, PlayStation had made videogaming a lifestyle.

Tomb Raider emerged from the UK Midlands in 1996, developed by Core Design in Derby. An innovative mix of large 3D worlds to play in, puzzles and combat, a detailed story and a new kind of leading character; it met

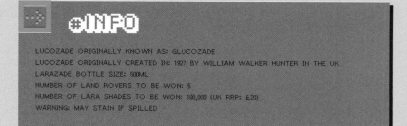

#INFO

LUCOZADE ORIGINALLY KNOWN AS: GLUCOZADE
LUCOZADE ORIGINALLY CREATED IN: 1927 BY WILLIAM WALKER HUNTER IN THE UK
LARAZADE BOTTLE SIZE: 500ML
NUMBER OF LAND ROVERS TO BE WON: 5
NUMBER OF LARA SHADES TO BE WON: 100,000 (UK RRP: £20)
WARNING: MAY STAIN IF SPILLED

with critical acclaim and captured the imagination of the world.

By the release of Tomb Raider II in 1997 (because of the success of the game, the developers were set upon a punishing sequel-schedule) Lara had already transcended her role as mere 'character in a videogame' – she was rapidly on a path to becoming a bona-fide cultural icon. Whilst other videogames cast plumbers, spaceships and soldiers as their protagonists, Lara was something conspicuously different. Such was the curiosity about her that she began to be written about by mainstream commentators, Douglas Coupland contributed to a book about her influence and then finally, in 1997, she emblazoned the cover of *The Face* magazine.

Lest we forget that Lara was also a powerful brand, product endorsement

deals marched alongside all of this. Seat cars and Landrover all invested in sponsorship deals with 'her', but it was energy-drink 'Lucozade' that provided the most memorable presence.

Tomb Raider started its relationship with Lucozade in the late 90s with a series of TV commercials placing the drink alongside Lara in a series of adventures. With the release of the first *Tomb Raider* movie in 2001, they decided to up the ante. For the first time in 70 years, the name of Lucozade was changed to underline their relationship. Thus, for three months 'Larazade' flooded the shelves of supermakets, taking the celebrity recognition of Tomb Raider even further into our domestic lives.

▶ Right: Larazade bottle (500ml).

045.

The Legend of Zelda:
Ocarina of Time 3D promotional Ocarina

2011

●INFO

WEIGHT: 95 GRAMS
NUMBER OF FINGER HOLES: 8 (TOP),
3 (BOTTOM)
DISTRIBUTED AT: GAMECITY 2011
'ZELDAY' ZELDA TAKEOVER DAY
TUNED TO: A
MATERIALS: PLASTIC

In 1998, Nintendo released one of the most acclaimed videogames of all time. The Legend of Zelda: Ocarina of Time took Link and the mystical world of Hyrule and translated them from 2D to 3D. For players who had grown up with the Hero of Time, this was a bold, brave and ultimately triumphant translation. While we might be used to 3D Legend of Zelda today, the addition of an extra dimension by no means guaranteed success. Plenty of other game franchises had tried to make the leap with varying degrees of success. Sonic the Hedgehog's adventures in 3D, for instance, always struggled to capture the magic of the Mega Drive's gloriously 2D graphics and game-play. But Ocarina of Time was a different matter.

The storyline was complex, the characters well-drawn, and the world was believable and solid. Hyrule Field was a vast, sprawling expanse that took time to cross even with Epona your trusty steed helping out. Kokiri Forest felt welcoming and homely, while the Lost Woods were eerie and foreboding. The game was full of quests and side-quests, essential missions and unnecessary detail. You didn't think about non-linearity and complex branching storytelling because this felt like a believable world that you were absolutely and completely a part of.

Believable it certainly was, but it was also utterly and enchantingly magical. Key to the magic was the ability to time travel. Link could be old or young. This wasn't just about moving into the third dimension, this was also about travelling through the fourth. Child Link could plant seeds that would appear as fully grown plants or trees when Adult Link visited them. The Child/Adult Link mechanic wasn't just a curiosity, it was integral to the game, and solving puzzles across space and time was one of the game's master strokes.

And the titular ocarina was vital to this four dimensionality. By learning and playing different tunes on the instrument, Link could solve puzzles and, most importantly, travel through space and time. The ocarina is to The Legend of Zelda what the lightsabre is to Star Wars, or the wand is to Harry Potter. It is utterly potent and utterly iconic. In fact, the popularity of Ocarina of Time was such that music stores saw a pronounced spike in interest and sales of the instrument in the wake of the game's release. And so, for a brief moment at least, the piercing sound of "Three Blind Mice" on the recorder was replaced by attempts to pick out 'Zelda's Lullaby' on this brand new instrument. A proud boast, indeed.

Of course, the ocarina significantly predates The Legend of Zelda, and examples have been found dating back many centuries. Although there are a large number of styles of ocarina, the 'transverse' variety that is played with two hands and held horizontally is the most commonly depicted. This blue, plastic ocarina is a rather newer specimen and was produced by Nintendo as a promotional item to celebrate the release of the 3DS remake of Ocarina of Time. This particular instrument was part of a set given to visitors to the 2011 'Zelday' event held as part of the UK's GameCity festival.

▲ Above: Nintendo 3DS packaging (front).

▶ Right: The Legend of Zelda promotional ocarina.

046

LEGO
development wrap trophies
2008

Making videogames isn't easy. Making dazzlingly creative videogames with unrivalled wit, charm and downright playability is even less easy. It's worth reminding ourselves just how hard the process of making videogames is because when it's done well it seems almost natural. Game design decisions, characterisations, animations, sound effects and the feel of the controls in your hand, all seem obvious.

TT Games make it seem easy. Their playful reimaginings of the Star Wars, Indiana Jones, Marvel, Harry Potter, Lord of the Rings (etc...) universes are so perfect they almost look effortless.

But, of course, it is anything but. These are object lessons in masterful game design. And even though they are made of pixels and polygons, the virtual bricks of the LEGO videogames lose none of their plastic counterparts' weight, substance and, well, plasticity... Make no mistake, creating a matchless catalogue of LEGO videogames involves huge amounts of work and contributions from many people.

In recognition of this, these acrylic blocks are given to every team-member who's worked on each LEGO game. Of course, they stack and connect like LEGO bricks – monuments to each personal contribution.

And it's not just making videogames that is hard. These perfectly crafted trophies might look perfectly inevitable, but they too are the product of consideration, revision and creative endeavour. Head of Production, Jonathan Smith explains,

'Our first attempt to create some kind of trophy to acknowledge this contribution came at the end of LEGO Star Wars II; a print of the game cover with a short inscription. It was horrid. An advert for a pirated version of the game crossed with your worst wooden-framed imagining of an Employee of the Month Award.'

So with LEGO Indiana Jones underway, so was born the quest for a new trophy concept which could properly acknowledge and celebrate everyone's work.

'Associate Producer Luke Cashmore took up the challenge, coming up with the initial concept of a lucite block entombing a LEGO minifigure. Inspired by the always-expandable LEGO System itself, he proposed that these bricks would have locking studs on the top. (Luke soon moved over to Design, and went on to have a mountain named after him in LEGO City.)

The first prototype was commissioned from a manufacturer in Slough, local to our Publishing office – and it was immediately clear that we had a worthy platform for the many celebratory awards to follow. Indy stood upright and smiling in his plastic display as the perfect icon of the pride felt by the whole team. Ten years on, the trophies are manufactured by the same supplier with team members able to choose from a selection of encased figures as each project is completed. It is an indication of their prolific output and success that everyone now has their own unique personalised desk-tower of plastic bricks reminding them of their achievements, privilege and excellent fortune,'

....

▲ Above: Assorted wrap trophies.

▶ Right: Wrap trophies for LEGO Batman and Harry Potter Years 1–4.

047.

LEGO Minecraft

2012

⊕INFO

LEGO PRODUCT NUMBER: 21102
INCLUDED MICRO MOBS: 2 (STEVE AND CREEPER)
RELEASED: 1 JUNE 2012
ORIGINAL PRICE: £34,99/$34,99
LEGO PRODUCT STATUS: RETIRED

It is often said that Minecraft is like a digital version of LEGO – albeit a LEGO set with an almost limitless supply of building materials. Well, here things come full-circle as the digital re-enters the analogue world and pixel blocks become plastic bricks. And there's no pickaxe required.

There have been a number of LEGO Minecraft sets, each modelling different landscapes and locales familiar from Mojang's phenomenally successful game. The first set was released in 2012, with two further sets based on 'The Nether' and 'The Village' announced the following year. Seven more including 'The End', 'The First Night' and 'The Ender Dragon' arrived by the end of 2014. These original sets were part of the 'Microworlds' series, which is based around the smallest LEGO unit – a single stud – making for a miniaturized but perfectly pixelated recreation of Markus Persson's masterpiece for your dining-room table. The Micro World sets have since been discontinued (or 'retired' as LEGO put it) and command pretty steep prices on auction sites. Their appeal to both LEGO collectors and Minecraft fans makes them very desirable pieces.

Later in 2014, minifigure-sized LEGO Minecraft sets were

announced. There are plenty to choose from here as well, with The Ocean Monuments, The Jungle, and The Desert Outpost all vying for attention – and money. And of course, each set comes with some of your favourite – and most feared – characters immortalized in minifig form. There's Alex and Steve, a selection of farm animals including Pigs and Sheep, and of course, a host of mobs from Skeletons to Zombies, Iron and Snow Golems and, of course, the dreaded Creepers. And carrots. Lots of carrots.

While you can reconfigure the sets and mix them up any way you choose – even mixing them with other sets (Star Wars Minecraft,

anyone?) – it is perhaps a little ironic that Minecraft notoriously gives players little in the way of instructions as to how to survive the first night, let alone how or what to build, while the physical LEGO Minecraft bricks all come with lavishly illustrated instruction manuals that carefully detail each step of the build. That almost sounds like the plot for a film. An AWESOME film.

▲ Above: LEGO Minecraft packaging and brick sacks.

▶ Right: LEGO Minecraft model (built).

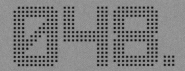

048.
Lemmings Adventure Gamebooks
1991

●INFO

NUMBER OF BOOKS IN SERIES: 2
PUBLISHER: PUFFIN
AUTHORS: NIGEL GROSS AND
JON SUTHERLAND
NUMBER OF PAGES:
THE GENESIS QUEST — 192; THE HYPNOSIS
ENIGMA — 176
WEIGHT: THE GENESIS QUEST — 112 GRAMS;
THE HYPNOSIS ENIGMA — 102 GRAMS

DMA Design's Lemmings series were among the most popular games of their time, and there can have been few Amiga or PC gamers who didn't spend days, weeks and months trying to guide their tribes to safety through treacherous terrain and a sometimes suicidal desire to self-destruct. Lemmings was part-platform game and part-puzzle game. In fact, so popular was the game that it has been ported to almost every conceivable gaming console or computer platform, to ensure that the widest possible audience can enjoy and endure the agony and ecstasy of creating a safe passage for a group of lovably hapless creatures determined to seemingly seek out their own demise.

Of course, Lemmings wasn't only ported to computer platforms and consoles. It was also ported to paper. These gamebooks take the back-story and premise of the Lemmings game play and meld it with the choose-your-own adventure books pioneered by Edward Packard with *The Cave of Time* and the *Fighting Fantasy* series penned by Ian Livingstone and Steve Jackson.

There were just two books in the Lemmings Adventure Gamebook series. Written by Nigel Gross and Jon Sutherland, *The Genesis Quest* and *The Hypnosis Enigma* are both set within the world of the Lemmings 2 videogame, being set on Lemmings Island. However, while it is possible to deduce this connection from the books' setting, it is surprising just how little reference is made to the videogames.

For sure, the books only exist because of the Lemmings videogames, but if you imagine these books being written and published 30 years later, it's hard to think they wouldn't be full of adverts for existing and forthcoming games. The publishers would, no doubt, want the readers to think they were in the middle of an innovative trans-media storytelling system, even though readers might have a nagging doubt that this was actually a way of cross-promoting products and driving sales. But it is striking how little of this there is here. These don't read as adverts for the Lemmings universe of products, these are adventures lovingly crafted within the Lemmings world.

There are no announcements of soon-to-be-released games. No full-page adverts for other merchandise. Instead, what we have are two gamebooks full of puzzles inspired by the Lemmings videogame and brought to life with page-turning puzzles and black and white artwork. The choose-your-own-adventuring doesn't reach the same levels of sophistication as *The Warlock of Firetop Mountain*, as the Lemmings gamebooks are quite simplistic and

don't have the multiplicity of routes or endings as Livingstone and Jackson's masterpieces, but these certainly are more than interesting curios in a marketing blitz.

Over the years, there have been numerous other print publications dedicated to Lemmings but these have mostly been strategy guides helping players to navigate their way through the fiendish puzzles in the digital games. As such, *The Genesis Quest* and *The Hypnosis Enigma* are unique in setting out new puzzles on paper and providing an analogue Lemmings experience.

▲ Above: Lemmings retail packaging.

▶ Right: The Genesis Quest' Lemmings Gamebook with detail of interior notes.

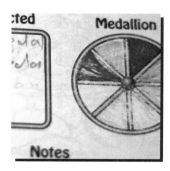

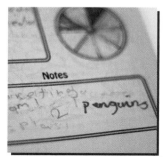

A Computer Owner's Guide To The Care Of And Communication With
LITTLE COMPUTER PEOPLE
1985

ALSO KNOWN AS: 'LCP' AND 'HOUSE-ON-A-DISK'

DESIGNED BY: DAVID CRANE AND RICH GOLD

JAPANESE PORT: 'APPLE TOWN STORY'

RELEASED BY: SQUARE IN 1987 FOR THE NINTENDO FAMICOM

ZZAP!64 MAGAZINE REVIEW SCORE (ISSUE 7, 1985): 97% 'A STUNNING ADVANCE IN COMPUTER ENTERTAINMENT'

Before the first Nintendog woofed, before The first Sim tried to get out of the swimming pool only to realize the player had removed the ladder, before the first Tamagotchi got into its spaceship and headed to Earth, there were the Little Computer People. Admit it, you always suspected there were little people living in there, didn't you? So did David Crane and Sam Nelson. But how to prove it?

After years of research, hard work and creative speculation, we invented what finally became the turning point in this arduous investigation: the 'House-On-A-Disk'.

So begins the 'Letter of Introduction' in the game's instruction manual. No wait, maybe game isn't the right word. It's more of a research project. And, come to think of it, its not an instruction manual. It's called 'A Computer Owner's Guide To Care Of And Communication With Little Computer People', and it's written by the Little Computer People Research Group. It even has space in the back to fill in your scientific observations. This is high concept stuff.

The Activision Little Computer People Discovery Kit, to give it its full name – or LCP as it was known by anybody in a hurry who didn't have time for that mouthful of a title – was truly ahead of its time. Although you would be forgiven for not thinking so on first inspection. Running the House-On-A-Disk for the first time, you are greeted with a representation of a living room, bathroom, bedroom, kitchen. It's all very nice. And it's all very empty. Almost eerily so. Almost boringly so.

But, after a few minutes, something appears. Somebody appears. Just like David, Neil and (go on, admit it) you suspected. There are people in here. Little people. Little Computer People. And they have a dog. If they both like the look of the place, they'll move in and you can give them a name and get to work.

As well as researching their behaviour, your role is to care for the LCP. You can arrange to have food delivered (Ctrl-F), you can fill their water tank (Ctrl-W), you can send dog food (Ctrl-D), and their facial expression will tell you how they're feeling. If you're concerned about your LCP's emotional wellbeing, you can boost their mood by sending a record to play, a book to read, or by playing a game with them. There's Card War, Anagrams and 5-Card Draw Poker to choose from. For a serious case of the blues, Ctrl-P pets your LCP, which, according to the existing research, they all seem to really enjoy.

If all this makes the LCP sound a bit needy, it shouldn't. They're perfectly capable of entertaining themselves. Their piano repertoire runs from Bach to Boogie-Woogie and, unsurprisingly, they love to play on their own little computers. Wait. Are there even Littler Computer People living in their computers? And what if they also had computers? Come to think of it, when you type Ctrl-C to phone them, the LCPs don't actually speak to you. But they definitely jabber away in an as-yet-undeciphered language to somebody. Maybe this is like Douglas Adams' *The Hitchhiker's Guide to the Galaxy*, and the LCPs are actually conducting research on us?

▲ Right: Owner's Guide for C64/128 disk version.

▶ Right: Retail packaging (C64/128 cassette version) with poster.

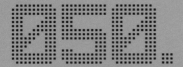

Little Professor

1976

eINFO

SUITABLE FOR AGES: 5–9

DISPLAY TYPE: LED

BOOK ENCLOSED:
FUN WITH MATH FACTS

RARITY STATUS AMONG CALCULATOR
COLLECTORS: VERY COMMON

BATTERY: 1X 9V

DIFFICULTY LEVELS: 4

ASSEMBLED: ITALY

Everybody knows that maths is important for videogames. Videogames are built on code. But what if the game wasn't just built on a foundation of maths? What if the game *was* maths? What if the gameplay was a series of addition, subtraction, multiplication and division problems? That's not too hard to imagine. There's a long tradition of puzzle games that require players to perform mental arithmetic and work with logic. Just look at Sirvo's smash hit 2014 puzzle game 'Threes!' for an example. This was a beautiful sliding block puzzle based around combining ever-increasing multiples. But it still had a beautiful puzzle game interface and focused in on a specific mathematical operation.

Imagine, instead, a game that didn't even attempt to dress up its mental arithmetic challenges as anything other than mental arithmetic challenges. Imagine a game where the challenges took the form of sums. And imagine that the gaming system you played on was explicitly modelled on a pocket calculator. Exactly the kind of pocket calculator that Gunpei Yokoi imaginatively turned into the Game & Watch. But here, it's just a calculator. Buttons for the numbers 0–9 and for plus, minus, division and multiplication, and a single line of red vacuum fluorescent display showing the digits.

Now imagine that when you turned on this game system/calculator and pressed 'Go', you were confronted with: '98+34='

What you're imagining is the Texas Instruments' Little Professor from 1976.

To be clear, there are no animations of cute characters, no sounds of any kind, just maths problems. If you get an answer wrong, you are presented with 'EEE' error message on the display, just as though you had entered an improper command like dividing by zero on a standard pocket calculator… and the question is restated with no further help or context. And things are not much better when you get the answers right! You simply move on to the next question. After ten questions, you are treated to a flashing number representing how many you got wrong (or reminding you of your failure).

But, it is all encased in bright yellow plastic with the kindly face of the character we assume to be the Little Professor peering over the pages of a book (the book we might also assume you should have read more carefully if you wanted to get that flashing '10'!)

The Little Professor wasn't the only Texas Instruments educational computer game. In 1978, the company released the Speak and Spell. Making use of its innovative speech synthesis technology, the Speak and Spell was

your own portable spelling bee. Spell 'Apple', it would demand, in its characteristically grungy but mostly intelligible computer voice.

While dedicated spelling and maths handhelds might have seen their heyday in the late 1970s and early 1980s, the legacy of Speak and Spell and Little Professor lives on in the 'Dr Kawashima's Brain Training: How Old is Your Brain?' series. For those seeking a purer mathematical update of the Little Professor, however, another high-ranking member of the Academy is at hand. 'Professor Kageyama's Maths Training: The Hundred Cell Calculation Method' could be just the thing to add to your collection.

▲ Above: The 'Little Professor'
created by Texas Instruments.

◀ Left: Speak & Spell included
speech synthesis.

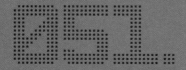

Magnavox Odyssey 1972

#INFO

RELEASED: 1972 (NORTH AMERICA), 1973 (EUROPE)
CONTROLLERS: TWO WIRED 'PADDLES'
MAXIMUM NUMBER OF DOTS SIMULTANEOUSLY DISPLAYED ON SCREEN: 3
ORIGINAL PRICE: $99
POWER: 6 X C TYPE BATTERIES OR OPTIONAL AC ADAPTER
PROTOTYPES: 'BROWN BOX' AND 'TV GAME #1'
PRE-RELEASE NAME: SKILL-O-VISION
THE 'SHOOTING GALLERY' GAME INCLUDED THE FIRST VIDEOGAME LIGHT GUN PERIPHERAL
ODYSSEY INVENTOR RALPH BAER WAS AWARDED THE US NATIONAL MEDAL OF TECHNOLOGY IN 2006

The title of 'the father of videogames' has been applied to a few people over the years. Atari's Nolan Bushnell and Nintendo's Shigeru Miyamoto being just two. But of all the contenders, Ralph H. Baer has the best claim to the title.

Baer was a prolific inventor creating, among other things, the sound and light pattern-matching game 'Simon'. However, his major contribution to videogames came in the form of the Magnavox Odyssey. The specifications don't sound too impressive on paper: the Odyssey couldn't display colour and had no sound capabilities of any kind. It could display one vertical line and three square dots on the TV screen it was connected to. You read that right, by the way. One line and three dots, not three beautifully-rendered characters, or three frames of animation. Three dots. And all drawn on screen in glorious black and white and in total silence. Two of the dots were controlled by the two players via their controllers and the third dot was controlled by the Odyssey itself. The vertical line was used to mark out the centre line of a tennis count, for example (you might even call it 'eye candy') Ralph Baer is the father of videogames, you say? Are you sure? Yes, definitely.

Simple though it might sound by today's standards, Baer's creation was utterly revolutionary because, before he put those three dots on the screen, there had been none. TV screens were resolutely non-interactive. You could shout at the characters in your favourite soap opera or game show as much as you liked but it didn't change a thing. With the Magnavox Odyssey, what Baer created was the first videogame console, and after May 1972, TV sets would never be the same again. The commercial videogame industry was born.

So, what made the Odyssey so special? It had two controllers reminding us that, from the very start, videogame play has been multiplayer and social. It was battery powered (and a set of batteries were actually included in the box!) It also had the capability to play different games. It was a console platform rather than a single-game device. New games were loaded by slotting in 'game cards'. Unlike the cartridges that Nintendo and Atari would use, the Odyssey's game cards had no fancy plastic cases or colourful labels and were instead bare printed circuit boards that modified the console's internal circuits when connected. Despite these differences in appearance and technology, the idea of the reconfigurable gaming console platform had arrived and the Odyssey paved the way for the generations of consoles we know today. In the US, the Odyssey was bundled with 13 games (10 in the international versions) with a total of 28 being released throughout the life of the system.

Not everything in the Odyssey package would be quite so familiar to videogame players today, however. Search through the box for your PlayStation. Xbox or Switch and you probably won't find dice or paper money. This is the sort of thing you'd more likely find accompanying a board game, so what's it doing shipping with a videogame console? The answer comes back to those three dots. If you're designing a tennis game, you have a dot for each player and a dot for the ball (all square, of course but who's complaining in 1972?) That doesn't leave any graphical power to draw scores or counters on screen and the Odyssey's diode logic circuits didn't give much scope for sophisticated game systems anyway. The solution to keeping score? Pencil and paper. What do you get for winning? Paper money. How do you decide who goes first? Roll the dice. Simple. Effective. Analogue.

The three dots also explain perhaps the most famous and inventive aspect of the Odyssey – the plastic overlays. These literally attached to the TV screen and transformed it from a football to a hockey pitch or from a roulette wheel to a haunted house.

▲ Above: Magnavox Odyssey and controller.

▶ Right: Instrument inspection card and TV screen overlay.

Mastering Pac-Man

1981

INFO

WRITTEN BY: KEN USTON
PUBLISHED: ECHO POINT BOOKS AND MEDIA
ORIGINALLY PUBLISHED: 1981
BOOK DEDICATED TO: RAE FOY AND ERROLL GARNER
PAGES: 128
CHAPTERS: 15

Simple to pick up, difficult to master. That's the watchword for countless games of the early 1980s. Pac-Man is a case in point. It has minimal controls with just a single joystick. There is a maze filled with dots to consume, and there are ghosts who chase after Pac-Man. Munching one of the four power pellets turns the tables and the hunter becomes the hunted. Turning blue, the ghosts are temporarily vulnerable to Pac-Man's ravenous gluttony. All of this is explained in a simple animation or 'attract sequence' that runs on a loop, both enticing the player to insert their coin and reassuring them that the game is almost comically straightforward.

Simple to pick up and play it may be, but difficult to master really is an understatement. Pac-Man is hard. Really hard. And you will always lose.

Because Pac-Man is hard, we're going to need some strategy. If we want to get beyond the first maze or two, we'll need more than swift reactions, and we definitely can't just rely on luck. Speak to a modern Pac-Master or read any of the detailed analyses of the games produced by players over the last decade or so, and Pac-Man reveals itself to be a game about the ghosts. Each ghost has its own personality. The red one really seems to have it in for Pac-Man and actively chases him down like a

homing missile. It's almost merciless. And the ghosts work together. If you think about it, it wouldn't be much fun if each ghost behaved in the same way. Imagine if they all just chased after Pac-Man. There would be a yellow disc followed by a line of four ghosts. They'd only catch him if they could run faster and that wouldn't be fair – or much fun. Toru Iwatani knew this and so each ghost actually has a different AI routine so they seek out Pac-Man in a different way and can appear to head him off in a pincer movement.

And so, for the modern Pac-Man player, this is a game about ghosts and AI. Learn these remarkably simple but fiendishly effective AI patterns and you can outsmart the ghosts.

If you were playing the game in the 1980s, Pac-Man was a different game. Not literally different, of course, it was the same code and the same AI routines, but it was played in a different way. In the 1980s, Pac-Man was all about the maze and the patterns the successful player had to learn were routes that charted safe passage. Players would practise and learn these routes and execute them with split second precision to move through the maze as if the ghosts weren't there. They were there, and they were chasing down Pac-Man in exactly the same way as before, but a successful

pattern meant that they might as well not be. Because the AI rules are so simple and the ghosts behave predictably to Pac-Man's movements, if the player takes the same route, the ghosts will move in the same way each and every time. If it worked last time, it will work this time.

So, how were these patterns discovered? It was pure trial and error. Players played and they died. They played and they won. And when they won, they wrote down the route they took and they practised it again and again. Played in this way, Pac-Man is as much a memory game as a maze game.

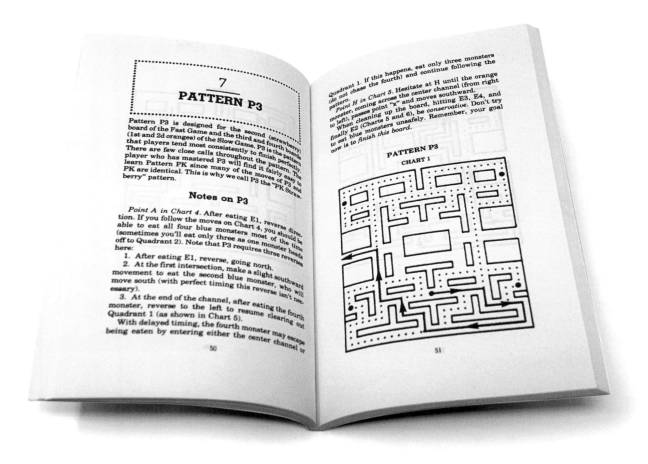

7
PATTERN P3

Pattern P3 is designed for the second (strawberry) board of the Fast Game and the third and fourth boards (1st and 2d oranges) of the Slow Game. P3 is the pattern that players tend most consistently to finish perfectly. There are few close calls throughout the pattern. The player who has mastered P3 will find it fairly easy to learn Pattern PK since many of the moves of P3 and PK are identical. This is why we call P3 the "PK Strawberry" pattern.

Notes on P3

Point A in Chart 4. After eating E1, reverse direction. If you follow the moves on Chart 4, you should be able to eat all four blue monsters most of the time (sometimes you'll eat only three as one monster heads off to Quadrant 2). Note that P3 requires three reverses here:

1. After eating E1, reverse, going north.
2. At the first intersection, make a slight southward movement to eat the second blue monster, who will move south (with perfect timing this reverse isn't necessary).
3. At the end of the channel, after eating the fourth monster, reverse to the left to resume clearing out Quadrant 1 (as shown in Chart 5).

With delayed timing, the fourth monster may escape being eaten by entering either the center channel or

50

Quadrant 1. If this happens, eat only three monsters (do not chase the fourth) and continue following the pattern.

Point H in Chart 5. Hesitate at H until the orange monster, coming across the center channel (from right to left), passes point "z" and moves southward. When cleaning up the board, hitting E3, E4, and finally E2 (Charts 5 and 6), be conservative. Don't try to eat blue monsters unsafely. Remember, your goal now is to *finish this board.*

PATTERN P3
CHART 1

51

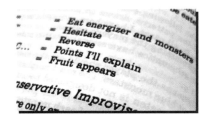

= Eat energizer and monsters
= Hesitate
= Reverse
= Points I'll explain
= Fruit appears

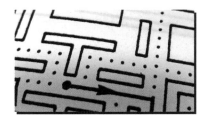

....

▲ Above (top): Chapter 7 opening of 'Master Pac-Man' book; (bottom) details showing movement in game.

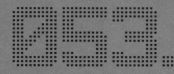

053.

Microsoft HoloLens

2016

#INFO

DEVELOPMENT CODENAME: PROJECT BARABOO
PRICE: $3000
OPERATING SYSTEM: WINDOWS MIXED REALITY
(WINDOWS 10)
INPUT SYSTEM: 'GGV' (GAZE, GESTURE AND VOICE)
WEIGHT: 579 GRAMS

At the time of writing, we might be reaching the end of the first flush (of the most recent flushes) of excitement about Virtual Reality. Domestic consumer demand, it seems, has fallen short of the expectations of the hardware manufacturers, which in turn has started to drive nervousness in developers. There's little point in making software for a platform if not enough people own one to buy enough copies. Early stage technologies are of course always beset with such risks.

Often mentioned in the same breath as VR is its close family member, AR (Augmented Reality). It's a technology about which everyone seems to be rather more confident, perhaps because it can gradually slide more easily into our lives than VR. When it gains traction, as it did with the sudden and dramatic explosion of Pokémon Go, it can be very persuasive.

Most of the mainstream bets around AR have so far been in smart phones and game consoles, but the more provocative and exciting interventions are happening in the 'wearable' space. Whilst no-one would argue that the Microsoft HoloLens is an everyday accessory yet, it starts to point towards a future of enhanced reality that feels within reach.

To use HoloLens is to see an overlay of the software output overlaid on the

space that you're physically inhabiting. Perhaps you'll be looking at a table top and see an object 'appear' on it in the lens. You'll then be able to walk around it, observe it in space, and potentially interact with it. It's a compelling proposition, and an exciting few minutes to experience as a technical demonstration, but we're yet to see how deeply AR will embed itself into our everyday lives. Pokémon Go worked fantastically well, but context is everything. Everyone already knows that millions of Pokémon are hiding everywhere in the world around us, waiting to be

discovered, captured and collected.

The potential for games and entertainment in AR is seemingly obvious. HoloLens and AR throw another fascinating potential onto the chaotic pile of things we might call videogames.

....

▲ Above:Examples of HoloLens application.

▶ Right: HoloLens mixed reality smartglasses.

Ming Micro: Portable 8-bit Video Synthesizer

2016

◈INFO

DESIGNED BY: DR JORDAN BARTEE
CREATED BY: SPECIAL STAGE SYSTEMS
AV OUTPUT: 240P NTSC VIDEO AND MONO
AUDIO ON PHONO JACKS
GRAPHICS ENGINE SPECIFICATION: 160X192 PIXEL
RESOLUTION, 4X4 SIMULTANEOUS COLOURS,
3 SPRITES WITH 32 BITMAPS
AUDIO ENGINE SPECIFICATION: 3 CHANNELS
(2 SQUARE WAVES, ONE DUAL MODE NOISE)
MIDI INPUT ON 5 PIN DIN CONNECTOR

8-bit graphics and bleepy-bloopy chiptunes – is anything quite so evocative of 'videogames'? It has been years since 8-bit consoles and computers were superseded by unimaginably more powerful systems capable of displaying billions of colours, full 3D graphics, and CD-quality audio in multichannel surround sound. Nonetheless, despite all the immeasurable advances, there remains something about the low resolution, blocky graphics, restricted colour palettes, and distinctly electronic sound, that says 'videogames'. Perhaps we seek out something characteristically 'gamey' because, over the decades, videogames have converged ever closer with film, taking their visual and sonic cues from blockbuster Hollywood cinema with epic camera work and orchestral scoring. Perhaps its simply nostalgia and an attempt to revisit childhood.

Either way, now the restrictions, limitations and frustrations have been lifted, why would anybody want to go back to having just a few sprites for characters, a limited selection of tiles to build backgrounds, and a couple of square waves for soundtrack and effects?

Fire up Game Maker Studio and you'll be almost overwhelmed by the available options for creating graphics and game-play logic. Start up GarageBand, Apple's free Mac/iOS Digital Audio Workstation and you'll find way more instruments, effects and processing options than were even imaginable in the wildest dreams of a 1980s composer. There's just so much choice.

And that's the problem. Freedom of choice can be creatively stifling. You spend so much time thinking about what's possible that you don't make things. You tinker without actually creating. Perhaps one of the reasons some developers, artists and musicians return to 8-bit graphics and sound is that they offer freedom from choice. Keep it simple.

Enter the Ming Micro. It's a complicated device dedicated to offering a simple set of tools for graphic artists, musicians, DJs, VJs. It's a retro audio synthesizer capable of making chiptune-style sounds and effects. But it's also a retro video synthesizer capable of creating and manipulating 8-bit graphics.

Hook the Ming Micro up to a standard USB controller and plug it into a TV and you have a complete retro audiovisual synth that allows real-time tweaking of sprites and backgrounds, psychedelic cycling through colour palettes, and all to the tune of gritty square waves. It's like somebody went back to 1985, took an NES and a Commodore 64, hotwired them, attached a USB port, SD card slot and a flux capacitor and sent them into the future (via the 1960s where it could hang out with the hippies on Haight Ashbury for a bit). If Morton Subotnick made videogames, he'd probably make them with the Ming Micro.

The Ming Micro is actually a smaller, digital version of Special Stage Systems' Ming Mecca system, which is designed to integrate with the kinds of modular synthesizers used by experimental musicians. With built-in physics, collision detection and even a module that allows an NES joypad to be connected, it's possible to use the Ming Mecca to create simple platform games – all manipulated and influenced by banks of oscillators and envelopes – and all in real time. Blocky, retro, and almost hallucinogenic, it's part 80s home computer revival, part Ken Kesey Acid Test.

▶ Right: Special Stage Systems Ming Micro board.

055.

MissingNo.
fan art

2018

#INFO

'MISSINGNO.' FAN ART CREATED BY: ISHADOWCAT
MEDIUM: HAMA BEADS
TOTAL NUMBER OF HAMA BEADS
IN 'MISSINGNO.': 1152
COLOURS: 4
THE HAMA COMPANY BEGAN MANUFACTURING
PLASTIC STRAWS IN DENMARK IN THE EARLY
1960S BEFORE DEVELOPING THE COLOURFUL
BEADS THAT ARE NOW SOLD IN MORE THAN 50
COUNTRIES. THE COMPANY NAME COMES FROM
THE FIRST LETTERS OF THEIR SURNAME AND FIRST
NAME OF FOUNDER MALTE HAANING.

You've tried to draw a game character, right? At some point during a boring lesson at school, or in a less-than-thrilling meeting, or just because you found yourself at a loose end, you've picked up a pen and tried to draw Pikachu, or Sonic, or Mario. We know you have because we have, too. That's what makes us videogame fans. We don't just play games, we get inspired to make new things – pictures, songs, or mash-up movies. And, those drawings in the back of your exercise book or scribbled in the margins of the meeting agenda, they make you a fan artist. Maybe not the greatest fan artist in the world, but a fan artist nonetheless.

But what to draw? Well, you could copy existing artwork from within the game or from the box art or marketing materials. You could refine your technique until you can draw a scene from Stardew Valley that is indistinguishable from the original. Or you could invent new characters. Just because the official Pokédex says there are only 720, why can't you bring some more Pokémon into the world? Perhaps that's what this fan artist has done here? After all, that Pokémon looks more like one of those awkward L-Shaped Tetris blocks than anything you might find in Vermillion City. So, it's a new Pokémon they've created?

Well, not quite. In fact, this is an example of a Pokémon you can find in the original Pokémon Red and Blue Game Boy games. So, what is this? An Easter Egg? A special prize for those completing the game in a particularly hard way? And, if it's in the game, why doesn't it appear in the Pokédex and why can't I buy a cuddly, plush toy if it?

OK, let's delve a bit deeper. So, there's seven Types of Pokémon including Water, Fire, Psychic and Electric but MissingNo. doesn't belong to any of those groups. MissingNo. is a 'Glitch Pokémon'. In case you're wondering whether Glitch Pokémon is an official Type, it isn't. Not according to Nintendo anyway. But Pokémon fans might not agree.

So, what is a Glitch Pokémon? Well, that name is a bit of a giveaway. 'MissingNo.' isn't really a name at all, it's some text used by the game's programmers to alert them that the Pokémon game has gone wrong. Imagine the situation – a player has gone into battle and the program randomly generates a number to see which Pokémon they'll be fighting against. But the number is too big and doesn't have a corresponding Pokémon. It's literally a 'Missing Number'. And what about the graphics? They're just a garbled mess of pixels. So, Glitch Pokémon.

But, even though Nintendo have issued statements confirming that MissingNo. isn't a real Pokémon and that the sequence of events that players worked out to trigger its appearance can cause the game to crash and lose all progress, fans want to believe! In a world of Legendary and Mystical creatures, why wouldn't there be Pokémon so secret even Nintendo don't know about them?!

And so, MissingNo. has become the subject of countless stories, songs and pictures explaining their origin and relationship to all the other Pokémon. This is what fans do. They investigate, explore and invent. Maybe next time somebody says videogames stifle creativity, you should show them your book of MissingNo. portraits and explain how a combination of imagination and code helped create a complex back-story for this programming error.

▶ Right: MissingNo. 'Glitch Pokémon' recreated in Hama Beads by iShadowCat.

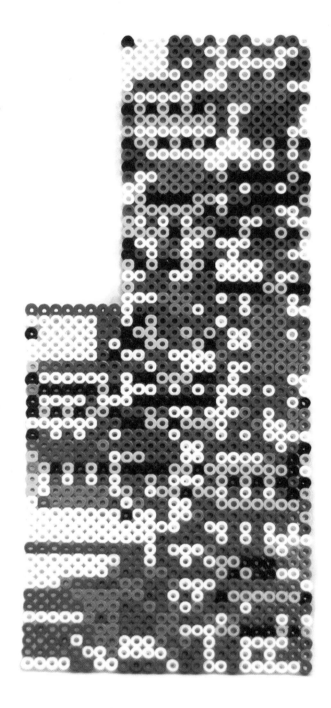

Mortal Kombat JAMMA board

1992

In the earliest days of coin-operated arcade games, each cabinet – and all the hardware inside it – was custom-made. So, if you wanted to update a game that wasn't as popular as expected or had run its course, the cabinet would go back to the manufacturer to be rebuilt. That's a lot of bespoke wiring and reconfiguration of power supplies, controller inputs and audiovisual components. And that's just the inside, as there's also graphics and artwork on the outside of the cabinet that needs to be changed to reflect the new game inside. With trends and fashions moving as fast as they did in the arcade business, this was costly and time consuming. The situation was really very similar to that seen in the home during the 1970s, where hardware systems dedicated to playing a single game dominated. Pong machines, Space Invaders machines, Astro Wars machines. By the late 1970s, the Fairchild Channel F and Atari 2600 pretty much put a stop to this by ushering in the age of the home videogame platform. These were general purpose videogame consoles that could be reprogrammed to play a wide range of different games which were distributed on interchangeable cartridges. We know what you're thinking: if only there was something like that for the arcade industry.

Well, you must have read the minds of the Japanese Amusement Machine and Marketing Association – or JAMMA as they're more usually called – because that's exactly what they were thinking, too. And so, in the mid-1980s, the JAMMA standard was announced and it completely transformed the arcade business. How so?

Most obviously, the JAMMA specification brought some standardization to arcade cabinet manufacture. It defined how power supplies and mounting harnesses should be fitted within the cabinet to connect displays, speakers and the control panel. But more importantly, by specifying the ways in which they communicated with the rest of the system, it defined the way the main printed circuit boards (PCBs) were designed. The PCB is what contains each game's special processors, memory and the program code that makes the game run. The PCB is effectively 'the game', and any PCB that was compatible with the JAMMA standard's pinouts could be fitted into any JAMMA-compatible cabinet. Essentially, the specification of this 56-pin edge connector created an industry standard arcade platform.

By separating the cabinet business from the PCB and game design business, the JAMMA standard allowed games to be changed and updated more easily and far more

#INFO

JAMMA NOW STANDS FOR: JAPAN AMUSEMENT MACHINE AND MARKETING ASSOCIATION (UNTIL APRIL 2012, IT STOOD FOR JAPAN AMUSEMENT MACHINERY MANUFACTURERS ASSOCIATION)

JAMMA PRIZE GUIDELINES: VALUE OF PRIZE ITEM MUST NOT EXCEED ¥800

MORTAL KOMBAT RELEASED: 8 OCTOBER 1992

CREATED BY: ED BOON AND JOHN TOBIAS

COIN-OP CONTROLS: 1 X 8-WAY JOYSTICK, FIVE BUTTONS (HIGH PUNCH, LOW PUNCH, HIGH KICK, LOW KICK, BLOCK)

'FINISH HIM' VOICE: PINBALL MACHINE DESIGNER STEVE RITCHIE

efficiently. As a result, rather than requiring cabinets to be shipped back to their manufacturers to be remade, new games could be sent out to arcade operators as conversion kits to be installed in the field.

Over the years, the JAMMA standard has been updated to accommodate new display and input technologies, but the principle of bringing the ease of plug-and-play game swapping remains one of the most important developments in arcade gaming. The JAMMA board pictured here is for Midway's Mortal Kombat game.

▶ Right: Mortal Kombat JAMMA Board (with incorrect spelling on the identification tag).

057.
Myst hint envelope
1993

#INFO

NUMBER OF HINTS: 3
INDIVIDUAL HINT SHEET DIMENSIONS: 210MM X 100MM
NUMBER OF BLANK PAGES AT BACK OF BOOK: 28
NUMBER OF LANGUAGES: 3 (GERMAN, ENGLISH, FRENCH)
FINAL WORD FOR EACH HINT: 'FLAP' (HINT 1), 'FLAP' (HINT 2), ''MAP' (HINT 3)

Multi-media CD-ROM's were once the hot new technology. Packages such as Macromedia Director gave designers the opportunity to bring interaction to people's screens using rich media in ways that hadn't been seen before. Encyclopaedias rushed to create CD-ROM editions, and books were issued with extra multi-media content, such as Bill Gates' *The Road Ahead*. Music albums had 'enhanced-content' added to them, which sprung to life when the CD was inserted into a home computer. If Microsoft's Encarta was the poster-child for the worthy use of this technology, then Cyan Worlds' Myst must surely be considered the signature work of entertainment software.

Myst was one of the first games that it was okay for middle-class adults to admit to playing. Self-consciously, even achingly slow to play, it communicated its own seriousness with great care. Fully embracing the new-found capability of the Compact Disc, it delivered megabytes of carefully rendered landscape artwork and video to the player. Its aesthetic was unique in videogames, as was its pace. Everything about it said 'grown-up' –

the pace came in for some criticism from some quarters, who described the game as a 'playable screensaver'.

Myst was at pains to project its literary credentials. Its puzzles were carefully constructed around the central location of a library, to which the player repeatedly had to return. It was also utterly uncompromising in its difficulty, to the frustration of many players.

In a nod back to the tradition of 'pack-in' materials established by the Infocom adventures of the 1980s, Myst further underlined its literary ambitions with the inclusion of a player journal and a sealed envelope inside its packaging. Players were encouraged to take notes as they progressed through the game, recording them in the blank journal for future reference. Its insistence on making this note-taking external to the game encouraged the player to take the adventure seriously, and also stripped the on-screen action of any supporting interface. The game only offered the player their view and their cursor to move over it. As people became stuck, they might finally resort to the sealed envelope. Written on the outside of it was the warning,

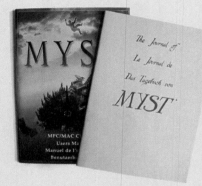

'Don't open unless you're really stuck!' On the inside, there were three hints to help the player progress.

Myst was one of the last gasps of pack-in materials, modest in comparison to the more audacious Infocom boxes. Nonetheless, it neatly drew a line between the action in-game and its literary pretensions. Despite being one of the key drivers of CD-ROM sales with its extraordinary commercial success, it felt wholly right for it to be shipped with paper.

▲ Above: Myst manual and player journal.

▶ Right: An unopened Myst hint envelope.

WARNING!

Three MYST® hints inside.
*Open **only** if in dire need...*

ATTENTION !

Trois astuces MYST® à
l'intérieur.
*N'ouvrir qu'en cas d'**extrême***
nécessité...

WARNUNG!

Drei wichtige MYST®-Hinweise.
***Nur** im äußersten Notfall*
öffnen...

RBB017RCX(2)

058.

NiGHTS Into Dreams
3D Control Pad

1996

When Sega announced its Saturn console would launch in 1994 in Japan, one thing was certain – there would be a new Sonic the Hedgehog game. The real question was whether it would be an old-school Mega Drive style 2D game, or if Sonic would make the leap into 3D just like Super Mario had done when he leapt from the SNES to the Nintendo 64.

What nobody expected was there wouldn't be a true Sonic game on the Saturn at all. OK, there was Sonic R developed jointly by Sonic Team and Traveller's Tales, but that was really more of a racing game than a continuation of Sonic's earlier platforming adventures.

What Saturn owners may not have realised however, was that the Sonic Team, creators of the original Mega Drive hedgehog, were hard at work on a new game. They were literally working day and night (Sega's offices had no soundproof rooms, so they had to record dialogue at night when there was nobody about). The game in question was Nights: Into Dreams, and it was set in the world of Nightopia where the evil Wizeman had to be defeated to bring order back to the world. Taking control of either Claris or Elliot, the player was guided around the dream world by the mysterious, impish Nights. Sounded exciting.

Looking at Nights as a spectator, you would almost certainly describe it as a 3D game. The world of Nightopia is beautifully rendered in 3D polygonal graphics, and the player taking on the character of Nights effortlessly glides into and out of the screen as they weave around collecting items and performing balletic aerobatics. Although the speed and grace are still there, it looks a long way from Sonic the Hedgehog's 2D game play where levels scroll from right to left and our blue avatar is locked to a single plane of movement.

Play Nights, however, and you find that your balletic path through the rendered 3D world is predefined. In fact, you are effectively flying along on rails. You can go backwards or forwards along the path, but you can't stray from it. Unlike Super Mario 64's game engine and camera system that allowed Mario to roam around the Castle grounds and beyond, Nights will always fly into or out of the screen at the point dictated by the flight-path.

And it is for this reason that Nights is both a 2D and a 3D game. It has 3D visuals and a richly drawn 3D world but its game play is resolutely 2D and, in this way, has more in common with Mega Drive Sonic than N64 Mario. But this was all by design. Sonic Team

PRODUCER: YUJI NAKA
PLAYABLE CHARACTERS: ELLIOT EDWARDS,
CLARIS SINCLAIR
NICKNAME FOR 3D JOYPAD: THE SPIELBERG
CONTROLLER
CHRISTMAS NIGHTS INTO DREAMS RELEASED:
DECEMBER 1996
DEVELOPMENT TEAM SIZE:
7 GROWING TO 20

had experimented with full 3D during Nights' development, but concluded that the game became too difficult to control.

One area in which Nights does more closely resemble Super Mario 64, however, is in its controller. Where Mario was developed alongside the new Nintendo 64 console and joypad, Sonic Team realised the limitations of the standard Saturn pad and designed a new one, the Spielberg pad, with an analogue stick and triggers. Why is it called the Spielberg pad? Well, that's because Stephen Spielberg was the first person outside the development team to play Nights and use the new controller when he visited Sega.

◀ Right (top): 3D Control pad unit.

▶ Right (bottom): Original packaging.

Nintendo 3DS
AR cards

2011

In all the excitement surrounding Nintendo's release of the 3DS handheld – all the speculation about convincing 3D effects that didn't require cumbersome glasses – one thing got slightly overlooked. Unpack the 3DS and you find the shiny, new console itself along with its curiously old-fashioned stylus input device, and the usual bundle of instruction booklets, safety guides and warranty cards. But nestling in the box is a cardboard folder. You think it would be hard to miss given that it is bright yellow, as we're dealing with a brand new console, you could be forgiven for setting it aside with the rest of the paperwork.

So, what's in this folder? The label on the front isn't hugely informative. 'AR Games Augmented Reality AR Cards' it says, along with some handy advice: 'Keep these in a safe place so you don't lose them!' To be honest, that's pretty good advice in general and probably could be extended to the 3DS console – and definitely the stylus, which never seems to be in its little cubby hole on the console when you need it.

Opening the folder, we find six playing cards. Blank on one side, each has a distinctive Nintendo design on

the other. There's a Question Mark block; three Pikmin; Samus from Metroid; Kirby; Link from the Legend of Zelda and, of course, Super Mario. That's a nice little extra. Not quite enough for a game of poker, but nice nonetheless.

But these aren't just ordinary cards. These are AR cards. Augmented Reality cards. These are cards designed to work with the AR Games application that is pre-installed on the 3DS. By placing the cards face up on a surface and pointing the 3DS' camera at them, you see on the screen a live view of your surroundings with 3D computer-generated Nintendo characters sprouting out of the cards as if by magic. You can make Mario sit on your dining room table, have Link on your kitchen counter, and balance red, blue and yellow Pikmin on your head. The Question Mark block reveals a box that opens up with targets to shoot using the 3DS' motion controls.

And if you didn't follow the folder's advice, you can download replacement cards from Nintendo's website as PDFs. Better still, because the size of the computer-generated character is directly related to the size of the AR card, printing out the PDFs larger than the original cards gives you even

bigger Pikmin to balance on your head.

Bundling playing cards with a videogame console might seem strange (although look at the amount of stuff that came with the Magnavox Odyssey, the first ever videogame console). But, when we bear in mind that long before it was a videogame company, Nintendo manufactured Hanafuda playing cards, it all starts to make a lot more sense.

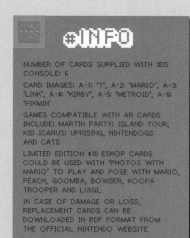

•INFO

NUMBER OF CARDS SUPPLIED WITH 3DS CONSOLE: 6

CARD IMAGES: A-1: '?', A-2: 'MARIO', A-3: 'LINK', A-4: 'KIRBY', A-5: 'METROID', A-6: 'PIKMIN'

GAMES COMPATIBLE WITH AR CARDS INCLUDE: MARTIN PARTY: ISLAND TOUR, KID ICARUS: UPRISING, NINTENDOGS AND CATS

LIMITED EDITION $10 ESHOP CARDS COULD BE USED WITH 'PHOTOS WITH MARIO' TO PLAY AND POSE WITH MARIO, PEACH, GOOMBA, BOWSER, KOOPA TROOPER AND LUIGI.

IN CASE OF DAMAGE OR LOSS, REPLACEMENT CARDS CAN BE DOWNLOADED IN PDF FORMAT FROM THE OFFICIAL NINTENDO WEBSITE

▶ Right: Nintendo 3DS AR cards, with front and rear detail of envelope.

Nintendo development kits

1995-2001

Ever wonder how games are developed when the final consoles haven't gone into production? Ever wonder how videogames are developed when the final specification of the system hasn't actually been finalized? Wonder no more. Here we have four pieces of hardware that help tell the story. These Test Kits and Development Units are among the tools that developers working on what would become Nintendo's GameCube and Nintendo 64 consoles would have used prior to the systems' release.

GameCube NPDP-GDEV

Before it was released to the public, the Nintendo GameCube was known as the 'Dolphin'. This 'NPDP-GDEV' unit was used by developers to create games for the system. It includes four controller ports but not the optical drive that the final GameCube hardware would use. Instead, games are stored and loaded on NPDP cartridges which actually contain a hard drive with enough storage for four games and which emulate the console optical disc system.

Nintendo GameCube Test Kit

Console Test Kits are special versions of the hardware used to play games while they're still in development. They run games from writeable media which don't go through the console manufacturer's production process for retail releases. This green unit was used by the development and quality assurance team at Traveller's Tales to test the GameCube version of the original LEGO Star Wars videogame.

Nintendo Dolphin NPDP Reader

The NPDP Reader is a special version of the GameCube console which was used during the game development process. It was primarily used for alpha and beta testing to identify bugs and glitches that needed to be fixed before a game was released. In place of the final GameCube console's optical drive, the NPDP Reader has a cartridge slot which accepts the hard disk-based NPDP cartridges that games were shared on during development. NPDP cartridges contain enough storage for four different games, or different builds of games, which can be selected with buttons on the edge of the case.

Bung Enterprises N64 Dev Unit

The Doctor V64 is a development and backup device made by Bung Enterprises that is used in conjunction with the Nintendo 64 console. The

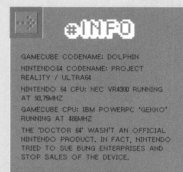

#INFO

GAMECUBE CODENAME: DOLPHIN

NINTENDO 64 CODENAME: PROJECT REALITY / ULTRA64

NINTENDO 64 CPU: NEC VR4300 RUNNING AT 93.75MHZ

GAMECUBE CPU: IBM POWERPC 'GEKKO' RUNNING AT 486MHZ

THE 'DOCTOR 64' WASN'T AN OFFICIAL NINTENDO PRODUCT. IN FACT, NINTENDO TRIED TO SUE BUNG ENTERPRISES AND STOP SALES OF THE DEVICE.

Doctor V64 unit was the first commercially available backup device for the Nintendo 64 unit. Although the V64 was sold as a development tool, it could be modified to enable the creation and use of commercial game 'backups'. Unlike official development units, the purchase of V64s was not restricted to licensed developers.

▶ Right: (top left) Bung Enterprises Doctor V64 and 512mb flash cartridge. (top right) Nintendo GameCube test kit, (bottom right) Nintendo NPDP-GDEV (bottom left) and Dolphin NPDP Reader.

061.
Nintendo DS
2004

+INFO

NUMBER OF DISPLAYS: 2 X TFT (THIN FILM TRANSISTOR)
TOUCHSCREEN TECHNOLOGY: RESISTIVE
MANUFACTURER: FOXCONN
DEVELOPMENT CODENAME: NITRO
ORIGINAL PRICE: £99.99 / $149.99
SOUND: STEREO AND VIRTUAL SURROUND
MICROPHONE: BUILT-IN
DIMENSIONS: 148.7 MM (W) × 84.7 MM (D) × 28.9 MM (H)

The first time Nintendo showed off its new handheld console in the early 2000s, there was some confusion. Was it really new? It looked kind of futuristic and it had a touch screen. But it also looked really familiar. In fact, it looked kind of old.

The truth is that the DS was really neither old nor new because it was both. It was new in that it made use of novel technologies and interfaces and included Wi-Fi, a touchscreen with a stylus, a microphone, stereo speakers with virtual surround sound, and dual screens (hence the 'DS' name). But it also had a directional pad on the left of the unit, some round buttons on the front face, and shoulder buttons on the top edge, just like a Super Nintendo controller from the 1990s. And it had a microphone, just like the original early 1980s Famicom controller, and dual screens just like the Game & Watch series from the even earlier 1980s. Much of this had been seen before in other Nintendo consoles and game systems – it even had backwards compatibility with the Game Boy Advance – but these things hadn't been put together in this combination before. And that was what was new.

Putting everything together in a clamshell case that immediately evoked the 'Multi Screen' Game & Watch games like Donkey Kong and Oil Panic sealed the deal (and had been employed in the Game Boy Advance SP). This was not just a Nintendo game system. This was a system made of Nintendo game systems.

You could say it was Nintendo drawing on its corporate design history. You could say it was Nintendo celebrating its past. You could even say it was another example of Nintendo's ethos of 'lateral thinking with withered technology' which had given rise to the original Game & Watch system. But you'd be hard-pressed to say it was backwards-looking. This was, for all its historical reference points, an exciting, different, and above all new system.

To be totally honest, the first raft of titles didn't necessarily showcase the system as well as they might. There was a conversion of the much-lauded Super Mario 64, which added Luigi and Yoshi to the mix and could be controlled with a curious plastic nub attached to the wrist strap which was somewhat less precise than the old N64 controller's analogue stick. Other titles such as Yoshi Touch and Go were effectively technology demos designed to show off the stylus, dual screen setup and microphone (which you could blow into to disperse clouds).

However, the system soon found its feet, and went on to be a huge success for Nintendo. In keeping with the system's design, games would include a mix of new and old franchises with Super Mario, Metroid, Pokémon and Zelda joined by Nintendogs and Dr Kawashima's Brain Training.

Like the Game Boy before it, the DS went through a number of incarnations with slimmer 'Lite' versions, a brighter-screened DSi and a bigger-screened DSi XL making up the DS 'family'. Between 2004 and 2014, the DS family sold more than 150 million units, making it the bestselling handheld console and second bestselling console ever (after the PlayStation 2). Not at all bad for an old system.

▲ Above: Detail of D-pad.

▶ Right: Original Nintendo DS hardware.

062.

Nintendo Entertainment System (signed by Masayuki Uemura)

1983

For one of the most important videogame consoles of all time, it sure has a lot of names. The Nintendo Entertainment System (or NES as it is often abbreviated) was originally released in Japan in 1983 under the name 'Family Computer', or Famicom for short, or F.C for even shorter! And, if that wasn't confusing enough, in South Korea, it was renamed the Comboy.

The NES and Famicom differ significantly in their outward appearance, with the former being the large grey box with slot-loading cartridge port and the latter an altogether more colourful affair with red controllers hardwired to the console that, when not in use, can be stored either side of the console's top-mounted cartridge slot. On the inside, however, things are the same. There's an 8-bit processor which has more than a passing similarity to the one powering the Commodore 64 and Apple II, custom sound and graphics processors, an expansion port and that all-important cartridge slot.

The system was designed by Nintendo's Masayuki Uemura under the code name 'GameCom' (there's another name to add to the list – it was, in fact, Uemura's wife who suggested 'Famicom') and after a rocky start involving a recall when a batch of faulty chips caused the

system to crash, it soon became the bestselling videogame console in Japan. The NES pictured here was signed by Uemura himself as part of the 30th anniversary celebrations held at the National Videogame Arcade.

Getting into the US was a little more difficult, however. A distribution deal with Atari broke down just before the console was due to be announced and, worse still, the US videogame market had nosedived in 1983, leaving investors, retailers and consumers wary. If videogames were a passing fad, Nintendo made sure its NES at least sounded different. This was an 'entertainment system', after all. It was a Control Deck, not a videogame console, and those things that looked like cartridges, they were actually Game Paks. To showcase Nintendo's technological innovation, a number of peripherals were released to support new kinds of game-play. These included a light gun – called the Zapper – and R.O.B. (The Robotic Operating Buddy, also known as the Family Computer Robot in Japan). As is often the case with peripherals, support wasn't exactly stellar, with only Gyromite and Stack-Up involving R.O.B. Of course, in the pantheon of less-than-successful NES peripherals, the crown surely must go to the Nintendo Power Glove. An ahead-of-

INFO

RELEASED: 1983 (JAPAN); 1985 (USA); 1987 (UK)
ALSO KNOWN AS: FAMICOM (JAPAN); COMBOY (KOREA)
PROCESSOR: RICOH 2A03
CONTROLLER PORTS: 2
CONTROLLER LAYOUT: D-PAD, A, B, START, SELECT
LOCKOUT CHIP: 10NES
STANDARD DISPLAY RESOLUTION: 256 X 240 PIXELS

its-time virtual reality input device with which you control game-play by moving your hand as if by magic? Perhaps. Wrist-achingly imprecise? Definitely.

Nonetheless, the popularity of games such as Super Mario Bros., Duck Hunt and Metroid ensured that the NES would not only sell in huge quantities but would also help reinvigorate the US market. The NES was officially discontinued in Europe and the US in 1995, more than a decade after its initial release. That's not bad going for a game console – ahem, Entertainment System. Having said that, it looks positively short-term compared with the Famicom, which was still available in Japan until 2003 with Nintendo still repairing consoles until the end of 2007!

▲ Above: NES pad and Control Deck.

063

Nintendo
Game Boy

+INFO

AVAILABILITY: 1989—2003
CPU: SHARP LR35902 AT 4.19 MHZ
DEVELOPED: NINTENDO R&D 1
DISPLAY: 47 X 43MM
DISPLAY RESOLUTION: 160 X 144 PIXELS
FRAME RATE: 59.7 FRAMES PER SECOND
MODEL NUMBER: DMG-01 (DOT MATRIX GAME)
POWER: 4 X AA BATTERIES OR 6V DC (MIN 150 MA)
SPEAKER: MONO
HEADPHONE JACK: STEREO
DIMENSIONS: 90 MM (W) × 148 MM (H) × 32 MM (D)

Let's get a few facts and figures out of the way first. The Game Boy was first released in Japan in April 1989 and would stay on sale until it was officially discontinued in March 2003. Throughout this time, in all its difference guises (e.g. Game Boy Pocket, Game Boy Light, etc.) it sold 118.69 million units, making it the bestselling handheld console of all time – until Nintendo's own DS overtook it. These are impressively big numbers, for sure. A platform that lasts for 14 years and sells over 100 million is good going by anybody's standards. However, this isn't what's interesting about the Game Boy. These big numbers come about because of what's interesting about the Game Boy. And what's interesting about the Game Boy is not how revolutionary it was, or how it pushed back the boundaries of technology. Quite the opposite. What's really interesting about the Game Boy is how unoriginal it is.

OK, that needs some explaining – and it's absolutely not a criticism. In fact, it's precisely how Nintendo designed it. But, how could Nintendo's first handheld videogame console be unoriginal? Why would over 100 million people buy something unoriginal? It uses a completely different type of display from the company's earlier Game & Watch handhelds, and it includes a cartridge

slot, so where the Game & Watch was hardcoded for a single game, the Game Boy was a platform that could host hundreds of games on hundreds of different cartridges. That's all true – but let's dig a bit deeper.

The Game Boy's controls come straight from the Game & Watch via the Nintendo Entertainment System (aka 'Famicom' in Japan) home console. There's a D-Pad on the left for moving the player's character or vehicle, and two buttons on the right for jumping or firing, with Start and Select buttons in the middle for starting and, you guessed it, selecting things. These are definitely tried-and-tested Nintendo controls.

As for the display, it's a 47 x 43mm 160 x 144 pixel LCD that, in its first incarnations at least, displayed graphics in four shades of (greenish) grey. 1998's Game Boy Color, as the name suggests, added colour graphics capabilities (but even then, this was limited to only 10, 32 or 56 simultaneous on-screen colours). Game Boy sound was very similar to the NES as well, though slightly cut down. Music and effects were played through the monophonic speaker built into the unit, although plugging in headphones allowed stereo playback.

So, the Game Boy wasn't a revolutionary piece of technology, in the sense that nothing it introduced

hadn't already be seen before. And that was precisely what they set out to do. What Nintendo and their chief designer Gunpei Yokoi did was use existing technologies that were well-understood, mature and well-developed, and combine them in a completely innovative and revolutionary way. Yokoi called this technique 'lateral thinking with withered technology' to convey the idea of concentrating on finding new and exciting applications for comparatively old, reliable, and cheap, technologies. Rather than adding battery-killing high resolution colour displays, graphics and sound chips, the Game Boy brought together existing audiovisual, processing, interface and display technologies to create a wholly new and wholly original device.

So, in one sense it is unoriginal, but that is precisely the point. And that's what makes it such an original design and truly more than the sum of its parts. And, once you know about 'Lateral thinking with withered technology', it lets a lot of Nintendo's subsequent product designs and their apparent lack of interest in the technological 'arms race' of gaming make a lot more sense.

▶ Right (top): Nintendo Game Boy unit.

▶ Right (Bottom): Game Boy Carry case, showing accessories including screen magnifier.

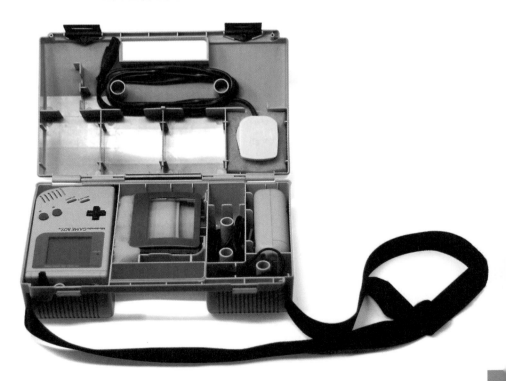

064.

Nintendo Game Boy Printer and Camera

1998

GAMEBOY PRINTER ALSO KNOWN AS:
POCKET PRINTER (JAPAN)
GAMEBOY PRINTER POWER REQUIREMENTS: 6 X AA BATTERIES
PAPER FORMAT: 38MM WIDE THERMAL WITH ADHESIVE BACKING
CMOS SENSOR: 128 X 128 PIXELS
SAVED IMAGE RESOLUTION: 128 X 112 (4 SHADES OF GREY)
IN 1999, THE GAMEBOY CAMERA WAS THE WORLD'S SMALLEST
DIGITAL CAMERA

In a world of smartphones, it's easy to take cameras for granted. Of course, there have been pocket and even disposable cameras for many decades, but the smartphone has not only given people high quality optics and image processing, but also has given them a camera to have with them all the time. And, let's face it, we really do mean all the time.

In 1998, digital cameras were bulky, expensive, and technically limited. For that matter, in 1998 mobile phones were bulky, expensive and technically limited too. Most people were still shooting with film and, if you had a mobile electronic device in your pocket, it was probably a games machine. In 1998, an inexpensive, high quality, portable digital camera would be a pretty big deal.

The device that Nintendo released as the Game Boy Camera was comparably inexpensive and definitely portable. It snapped into the Game Boy's cartridge slot, and peeped over the top like a modern-day webcam. But it definitely wasn't a high quality camera. And it wasn't intended to be. This was a very much a novelty.

The Game Boy Camera has a 128x128 pixel sensor (compare that with the many millions of pixels in a modern smartphone sensor) and captured in grainy black and white. Importantly, the Camera also came with software that, presaging contemporary photo editing and messaging apps, allowed the user to draw on or attach virtual stickers to their captured images.

It isn't just the low-resolution photos that remind us that the Game Boy Camera is a product of its time, Where many digital photos today are viewed on screens – whether the device on which they were taken, a computer monitor or a large screen TV in a living room – the Game Boy Camera was built with physical media in mind. It was made at a time when a 'photo' was a piece of paper you held in your hand, not a collection of pixels you pinched, zoomed and tagged. And so, alongside the Camera, the Game Boy Printer accessory allowed users to make hard copies of their original or edited creations.

The Game Boy Printer required six AA batteries and used a thermal printing process. As such, it could only print on special thermal paper, which was supplied on a 38mm wide reel that resembled a till roll and allowed over 100 photos to be printed. Although the Game Boy Printer was most commonly associated with the Game Boy Camera, a number of Game Boy cartridges supported the device and let players print out images from games.

With all the peripherals in tow (as well as a pocket full of spare batteries in case the Game Boy or Printer ran flat), you could be forgiven for wondering just how convenient and portable this really was. Certainly, Polaroid had been making instant cameras for many years – although you couldn't put virtual Pokémon stickers on people's faces with those before you printed them out which, for some photographers, was a big drawback.

Ultimately, with such a low resolution, the Game Boy is a long way from being a great camera. However, because capturing fleeting moments is key, there is an old adage in the world of photography that says the best camera is the one you have with you. On that basis, it's technically possible the Game Boy Camera could be the best, just as long as you left your smartphone at home.

◥ Right: Game Boy Camera (front and rear) and Game Boy Printer peripheral.

Nintendo Super Scope
(signed by Masayuki Uemura)

1992

#INFO

ALSO KNOWN AS: NINTENDO SCOPE
(IN EUROPE AND AUSTRALIA)

NUMBER OF PARTS: TWO (TRANSMITTER AND
RECEIVER)

INTENDED RANGE FROM TV SCREEN: 3 METRES

POWER: 6 X AA BATTERIES

COMPATIBLE WITH: SUPER NINTENDO
ENTERTAINMENT SYSTEM

CAMEO APPEARANCES IN: SUPER SMASH BROS.
BRAWL, SUPER SMASH BROS. MELEE

When it came to designing the Super Nintendo Entertainment System, everything had to be bigger and better than the NES. Everything had to be super. The graphics were improved, the sound was improved, even the console's look was altered. It was still pretty grey, but it was altogether more curvaceous than the angular NES, which had been modelled on a VHS player. And, of course, what console is complete without new controllers? The standard joypad that shipped with the NES added extra buttons. Where the NES pad had A and B buttons, the SNES added X and Y as well as two trigger buttons on the upper edge of the pad that soon became second nature to Super Mario Kart players power-sliding round corners and between obstacles.

And what of the much-loved NES Zapper? What would a Super Zapper look like? Well, it sure wouldn't look like a pistol. To be super, it would need to be big. Maybe something like a shoulder-mounted bazooka. And it would have a really substantial handgrip and a sight that the player looked through to aim. It would be a bit like the sort of thing Rambo would have. In fact, not just a bit like it, exactly like it. But in grey.

From a technical perspective, the Super Scope is actually very similar to the Zapper that preceded it, although where the pistol was tethered to the console like a standard joypad, the Scope was wireless. But the underlying technology is basically the same. Neither the Zapper or Super Scope are guns in the sense that they don't emit anything – bullets, shells or anything else. They rely on the peculiarities of 1980s/1990s Cathode Ray Tube (CRT) TVs that draw their image with an electron gun that moves across the screen progressively creating the picture as it does. All this movement is far too fast for humans to detect, so we see a continuous and moving image, but the combination of the light gun and NES/SNES can detect the position of the beam and work out whether the player is pointing their weapon at it. If they are, it's a hit; if not, they miss.

It's an ingenious and counter-intuitive system in which the light gun is actually a receiver and it is the television set firing out particles of light. And because it's a system that relies on the particular ways in which CRTs work, it's one that is becoming harder and harder to use. With the adoption of LCD screens, which draw their image in a completely different

way, light guns simply don't work. And so, while flat screens bring us HD, better colour reproduction, better viewing angles, and rid gaming and TV viewing of the blurriness and image ghosting that was the bane of CRT owners, it seals the fate of a whole genre of games. Zappers no longer zap, and the Super Scope becomes a lot less super once it's reduced to being a large grey tube you look through.

However, even if you don't fancy scouring thrift shops and auction sites for the last remaining CRTs, all is not lost and both the Zapper and Super Scope live on. Not only is the Super Scope immortalized in the live action Super Mario Bros. movie in which it is used by none other than King Koopa himself, but both the Zapper and Super Scope feature as weapons in the Super Smash Bros. series.

This UK Nintendo Scope is signed by Masayuki Uemura, Head of Nintendo R&D2, who designed the NES and SNES systems.

▶ Right (top): Instruction manual.

▶ Right (middle): The 'Transmitter' unit.

▶ Right (bottom): Retail packaging (PAL version).

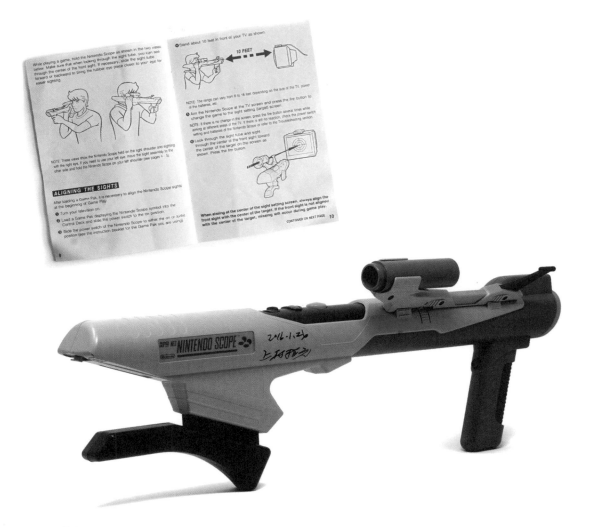

Nintendo Wii remote and accessories

2006

ALSO KNOWN AS: WIIMOTE
INPUT: ACCELEROMETER; INFRARED
SENSOR; D-PAD, A, B, +, -, HOME, 1, 2,
AND POWER BUTTONS.
WII MOTION PLUS ADDS: GYROSCOPE
CONNECTION: BLUETOOTH
POWER: 2XAA BATTERIES
ACCESSORIES INCLUDED WITH WII CONSOLE:
NUNCHUK AND WRISTSTRAP
OPTIONAL ACCESSORIES: STEERING
WHEEL ADAPTER, WII ZAPPER, GOLF
CLUB AND TENNIS RACKET ATTACHMENTS

Nintendo has always put a lot of thought and effort into its controllers. With the Game & Watch, it established the cross-shaped 'D-Pad' that has become a fixture of modern game pads. The SNES pad added shoulder buttons to the NES design. The N64 brought an analogue joystick, along with dedicated camera buttons for 3D games. The GameCube pad was an altogether more asymmetric affair with different clusters of buttons, two analogue sticks and combined analogue triggers and switches where the SNES' shoulder buttons had been. Before the Wii was released in 2006, speculation mounted as to what Nintendo would add to the control pad this time.

Far from adding buttons, the Wii Remote took them away. In fact, the Wii Remote didn't even look like a joypad. It didn't have multiple analogue sticks, or triggers, or clusters of multicoloured camera buttons. It wasn't even the same shape as a joypad. It didn't have handgrips or triggers. It looked more like a television remote. And this was exactly the intention.

Nintendo's argument was that videogame controllers had become too complicated, and this was causing a problem for new players. All those buttons and sticks were off-putting. So,

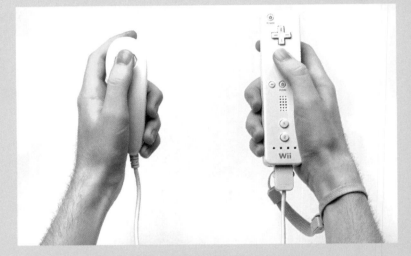

Nintendo built the Wii interface around the metaphor of the television. The controller was held like a TV remote control and pointed at the screen to make selections. The visual interface continued the TV metaphor with each game (or weather or photo application) being called a 'channel', represented by a little TV screen icon displaying the content. The idea was to simplify videogames, and what could be simpler than changing channels on a TV with a remote control?

Of course, the Wii Remote wasn't a standard TV remote control. For a start, it registered movement – and, if we want to know what Nintendo added to the Wii controller, it wasn't more buttons. It was motion control. This meant you didn't just vaguely wave it around somewhere in the vicinity of the TV to make selections, you actually pointed it at the screen and made selections by lining up the pointer and pressing 'A'. So, it was more like a TV remote crossed with a computer mouse crossed with a sprinkling of magic.

▲ Above: Wii Remote with nunchuck.

▶ Right: Wii Remote.

067

Noby Noby Boy
Papercraft

●INFO

NOBY NOBY BOY GAME DESIGNED BY:
KEITA TAKAHASHI
PLATFORMS: PLAYSTATION 3, IOS
PAPERCRAFT COPYRIGHT NBGI 2007
NUMBER OF STAGES IN MAKING PAPERCRAFT
BOY: 12
LENGTH OF COMPLETED BOY IN UNSTRETCHED
RESTING STATE: 280MM

It's tempting to think of game designers as being people who all trained in computer science. If not that, at least 3D modelling? There should definitely be computers involved, right? Perhaps not.

Videogames are a remarkably plural field, a chaotic meeting point of pretty much every creative discipline that has preceded it. Music, architecture, screenwriting, choreography, sound design; all these are skills that can be employed in the creation of a contemporary videogame. Computer Science binds them together, but it's not the pre-requisite for entry.

One of the key concerns of videogames, particularly since they extruded themselves into 3D, is space. I don't mean the infinite inky blackness above us, I mean the space around us. Games allow us to play with it, traverse it, jump through it, bend it to our will – it's no surprise then, that as a form they often attract people working in more physical fields.

Keita Takahashi trained in fine art, creating playful sculptural work before finding employment at Namco Bandai in Tokyo. It was there that he delivered his first game, Katamari Damacy. Twinning a simple art style with a fresh, very physical mechanic, Katamari became a cult hit around the world. Takahashi created an evocative world of colourful characters in simple

strokes, which made them ripe for cosplaying and fan-art tributes. The 'Cult of Katamari' exploded out of the Playstation 2 and into fan conventions around the globe.

By the time his next major project was announced, Keita was an acclaimed figure in the alternative gaming world. His work embraced a feeling of tactile play. Noby Noby Boy invited the player to push and pull a stretchy 'boy' character through the surreal world he shared with a host of other pastel-drawn friends. It was funny, fresh and suffused with a child-like innocence rarely seen in mass-market games.

Like Katamari before it, this was a friendly videogame. It was about taking part, about touching, about smiling and sharing. To help invite people into the world of Noby Noby Boy, Keita produced a series of 'paper craft' models and invited the public to create their own 'boys'. You could easily join in with the fun, but you had to sit down yourself and *make* it. In drawing a direct line between the world of the game and the homespun arts and crafts activity, Keita generated a warm glow around the world of Noby Noby Boy, using an extensive selection of marketing materials.

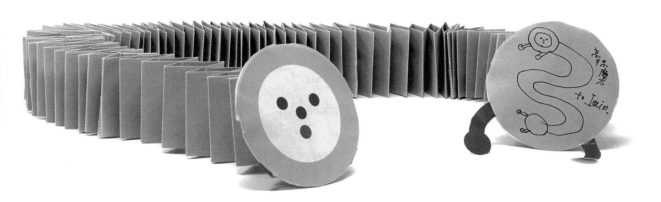

◀ Left: Noby Noby Boy papercraft net
(head and rear section).

▲ Above: Completed Noby Noby Boy
papercraft (by Keita Takahashi).

068.
Nokia
N-Gage
2003

●INFO

PROCESSOR: ARM920T AT 104 MHZ
AVAILABLE: 2003–2005
MEDIA FORMAT: MULTIMEDIACARD
DISPLAY ORIENTATION: VERTICAL
DISPLAY RESOLUTION: 176 X 208 PIXELS
OPERATING SYSTEM: SYMBIAN 6.1
ORIGINAL PRICE: $299
CAMERA: NO

Developed under the codename 'Starship', the Nokia N-Gage was released in 2003. It was among the first truly 'convergent' portable systems, combining the functionality of a number of different devices. It was a PDA (Personal Digital Assistant) that gave access to a calendar, To Do list and contacts, and it was an MP3 player but, most of all, it was a mobile phone and a handheld gaming console.

For a generation familiar with smartphones and effortlessly switching between Angry Birds, email and calling home, the N-Gage's combination of features might not seem groundbreaking. But it's worth remembering that when it was released the iPhone was still three years away, mobile handsets often had tiny black and white displays, and gaming on the go really meant the Game Boy Advance (which, while it let you play Yoshi's Island, didn't let you make phone calls!)

So, given how revolutionary it was, and given that Nokia were one of the major mobile handset manufacturers making some of the bestselling and best-loved phones at the time, why aren't we all carrying N-Gage 8s today?

Certainly, the N-Gage was ahead of its time in the way it brought together the worlds of gaming and mobile telephony. However, the problem was that it wasn't a very good gaming device or a very good phone. In fact, the N-Gage has become notorious for its unusual and esoteric design. For a start, there is no camera, so there's no photos or video. OK, not all mobile phones at the time had cameras, so maybe we can let that pass. It also looked like a taco, which was an odd choice, but who doesn't like tacos, right? Even if they're pressed up against your ear? Hmmm, maybe.

Less easy to overlook was the placement of the microphone and speaker. Because they were located on the edge of the device, it meant that using the N-Gage made you look like you had one huge ear! This earned the nickname 'sidetalking' which may sound cool, but in practice really wasn't. Mocking photos of people 'sidetalking' into book spines, pretzels, and even surfboards became suddenly popular (and are still easy to find by searching Google Images for the term). So, not a great phone from the company that had a reputation for making great phones.

What about gaming? It turned out that the N-Gage was not the most user-friendly gaming device either. Games were distributed on Mini Multimedia Cards (MMC) which were extremely small and neat. This meant that, unlike most mobile phones which had a few basic built-in games, the N-Gage could act as a platform more like the Game Boy. So far so good. The problem was that the card slot was located underneath the battery (yes, there was a time when phones had removable batteries!) Every time players wanted to play a different game, they had to remove the N-Gage's cover and battery compartment. In case you're wondering, this is not handy.

▲ Above: Screenshot of Tomb Raider from N-Gage.

◀ Right: Nokia N-Gage unit (top).

▶ Right: Tomb Raider Multimedia Card (MMC)

#INFO

OFFICIALLY LICENSED: YES
MATCHING TIE: SUPPLIED
TROUSERS: NON-PLEATED
SIZE: US 36-52
STYLE: SINGLE-BREASTED
CARE INSTRUCTIONS: HAND WASH COLD,
DRIP DRY, CAN ALSO BE DRY CLEANED.

You have your favourite blue Space Invaders T-Shirt. You have your trusty Pokémon socks with Charmander on them. You have your bright green Minecraft wristband with the Creeper face. And to top it all off, you have your Namco hat. You're definitely a gamer and, when it comes to smart-casual, you pretty much have things covered.

But what if the occasion calls for something more formal? What if you need to dress up? There's only one thing for it. You're going to need a Pac-Man tie. No, scratch that. If you're going to do something, do it properly or not at all. You're going to need a Pac-Man jacket, Pac-Man trousers and a Pac-Man tie.

There can be few people who don't immediately recognize Toru Iwatani's creation. Pac-Man really was the first truly global video-gaming icon. There had been popular videogames before Pac-Man, but they hadn't really had characters you could connect with. Pong had... the bats? Or maybe the ball? Space Invaders had aliens that looked like squid. And a spaceship. But Pac-Man was different.

Pac-Man had personality. Even the monsters had personality. They may have been out to get you, but they did it in such a cute way it was hard not to find them endearing. The game even had cut-scenes that fleshed out the

characters. The ghosts chase Pac-Man off screen, only for him to reappear supersized chasing them! A ghost chases Pac-Man but snags their robe and tears it revealing a... is that a leg underneath? This isn't Metal Gear Solid, but these cut-scenes develop the Pac-Man cast, morphing them from game play cursors to characters. They may not have been the most richly-drawn characters or have the most complex back-stories or motivations, but the *dramatis personae* of Pac-Man had undeniable charisma. And it didn't take long for marketers and merchandisers to catch on.

At the height of 'Pac-Mania', there was practically no item that was exempt from having Pac-Man's visage adorn it. Duvets, clocks, lunchboxes, moneyboxes, pyjamas, board games, hats, umbrellas... you name it, it probably had a Pac-Man on it. Appropriately enough for a character that was reportedly dreamt up when Iwatani saw a pizza with a slice missing, there was Pac-Man breakfast cereal, and even cans of Pac-Man macaroni cheese. You couldn't even turn on the radio to escape, because Jerry Buckner and Gary Garcia's 'Pac-Man Fever' reached number 9 in the US *Billboard* charts.

If you thought this was just a game, think again. And yet, even though at some point since the 1980s almost

everything has been consumed by the Pac-Man marketing machine, the sight of a Pac-Man jacket, Pac-Man trousers and a Pac-Man tie is still pretty remarkable. In fact, you might even call it 'a-maze-ing'.

▲▶ Above & right: Pac-Man suit and tie, and suit jacket details.

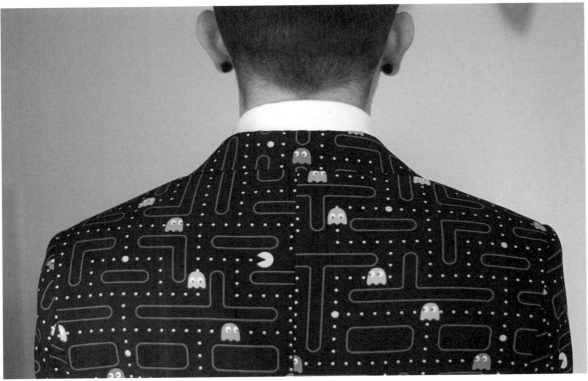

Pirate cassette inlays
1984-85

@INFO

SIDE A: THE WAY OF THE EXPLODING FIST
ORIGINALLY PUBLISHED BY: MELBOURNE HOUSE
RELEASED: 1985
SIDE B: DROPZONE
ORIGINALLY PUBLISHED BY: U.S. GOLD / MINDSCAPE
RELEASED: 1984
PIRATED ARTWORK MEDIUM: COLOURED PENS AND
BLACK BIRO

Let's get one thing clear, these are not the cassette inlays for Melbourne House's Way of the Exploding Fist or Hewson's Uridium. What gave it away? Was it the fact that they've been drawn using coloured pens? Or perhaps it was the handwritten instructions explaining the controls? Or maybe it was the, let's call it 'individual' approach to spelling? (or maybe the 'Fist' artist really means *objet* and is making a prescient statement about games' status as art?) You're right, it's probably just a spelling error.

They certainly look (a bit) like the original artworks; however, the fact is that, even though they bear the names of the games and the publishers, these are homemade, handmade facsimiles of the originals. For what purpose? Why would somebody go to such lengths? Perhaps these were made to replace the lost or damaged originals? That's a good and charitable – guess. But the truth is that these are homemade copies of the covers to accompany homemade copies of the games.

With games for computers like the Commodore 64 being distributed on cassette, making copies of them was as trivial as copying a Top 40 album.

Few people are likely to miss the 15-minute loading times they had to endure while their game loaded slowly – really slowly – from a cassette tape attached to their home Spectrum, C64 or ZX81, but it sure made copying and sharing games easier than with cartridge-based systems. The data on the game cassette tape was actually just recorded as audio, so any domestic hi-fi with tape-to-tape recording was a music and game-play duplication system. If you've ever heard the sound of a dial-up modem, you'll know the sound of computer data on cassette tape. It doesn't make for great listening, but it copies those bits and bytes just fine.

One thing these hand-drawn covers remind us of is that software piracy is far from being a modern problem. In fact, for as long as there's been software, there's been software piracy. And, for as long as there's been software piracy, there have been anti-piracy campaigns. It began with music, and in the UK, public awareness campaigns like 'Home Taping is Killing Music' sought to educate people as to how illegal duplication threatened the livelihoods of musicians.

In the UK, 'Home Taping' wasn't only 'Killing Music', but it threatened to do for games as well. Like many players at the time, the (anonymous) donor of this piece had duplicated a friend's copy of the game using nothing more than a domestic hi-fi. In the US, a later TV campaign aimed at young people and warning of the dangers of floppy disc duplication took a similar line – albeit with a so-bad-it's-good rap entitled 'Don't Copy That Floppy' that is quite possibly the most 1990s thing you'll ever see or hear. Be warned, it cannot be unseen or unheard (although, ironically, it can be viewed online, as various Internet users have made unauthorized copies of it!)

Alongside hotlines and education campaigns, a number of developers and publishers took more direct action. Some games prompted players to enter a specific word from their instruction manuals assuming that the prospect of photocopying vast reams of paper would be a disincentive. Other games relied on systems such as Software Projects' Software Copy Protection card which you can see on page 103.

▶ Right: Pirate cassette selection and detail of 'The Way of the Exploding Fist'.

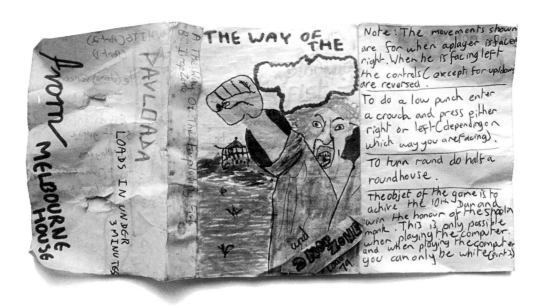

PocketC.H.I.P.

2015

+INFO

POCKET CHIP DISPLAY: 480 X 272 PIXELS
INTEGRATED STAND: NO (USE A #2 HB
PENCIL)
CPU: ARMV7 RUNNING AT 1GHZ
RAM: 512MB
PICO-8 VIRTUAL CONSOLE SPECS:
128X128 PIXEL DISPLAY, 16 COLOURS,
4-CHANNEL SOUND
MAXIMUM 'CARTRIDGE' SIZE: 32K

The PocketC.H.I.P. is a portable, battery-powered Linux computer built into a protective case with an integrated 480 x 272 resistive touchscreen, a QWERTY keyboard, Bluetooth and Wi-Fi connectivity and a battery that should power the device for about 5 hours. Developed by Next Thing Co., the PocketC.H.I.P. sells for around $70 (although you can pick up the C.H.I.P. computer without the display, battery or keyboard for just $9!). The PocketC.H.I.P. ships a host of software for programming and playing games so you can get up and running straight away. In fact, there are hundreds of community-made games to play, ranging from shooters to puzzlers to platformers. All with achingly retro chiptune soundtracks and graphics inspired by the 8-bit era of home computers and consoles.

OK, so a cheap computer with a stripped down, but nonetheless cool-looking, case with built in keyboard and display is really not that big a deal nowadays, even if it is really cheap (and really cool-looking). But it's not just the cost or convenience that make the PocketC.H.I.P. special; it's the fact that it ships with all the tools you need to make games as well as play them. Now, that is impressive for the price.

The real key to transforming the PocketC.H.I.P. into a game-making studio is a piece of software called PICO-8. This is essentially a 'virtual console platform'. What's that, you ask? Well, it basically defines a theoretical specification for an imaginary console and lets you design games for it on whichever device you run the PICO-8 software environment on.

The PICO-8 game engine is designed to be fairly basic, so that even people comparatively new to game design or coding can get to work and start designing new masterpieces. The platform specifies a 128 x 128 display with 16 colours (well within the PocketC.H.I.P.'s capabilities) and up to 128 8×8 sprites (a sprite is the computer graphics name for a moving element in a game such as a spaceship, the player's character or the enemies – basically everything that isn't the background!) This specification actually compares very favourably to most 8-bit systems of the 1980s, which could display only a fraction of the number of sprites often with far fewer colours simultaneously on screen, so there are bound to be some programmers from the 80s still telling you that you don't know how lucky you are!

With PICO-8 loaded, your PocketC.H.I.P. has everything you need to design the sprites, arrange your levels, and even create chiptunes-style music with the built-in Tracker-style sequencer (just like a Commodore Amiga musician would have used). Which is all very well, but where do you start? Where is that world-changing idea going to come from? Don't panic! Another neat feature of the PocketC.H.I.P./Pico-8 is that all those hundreds of community-made games can be edited and used as the basis for new creations. Alternatively, if you just want to make a game a little bit easier (or harder), you can tweak its parameters to make your custom version.

▲ Above & right: PICO-8 screenshots.

▶ Right: Pocket C.H.I.P. unit (top).

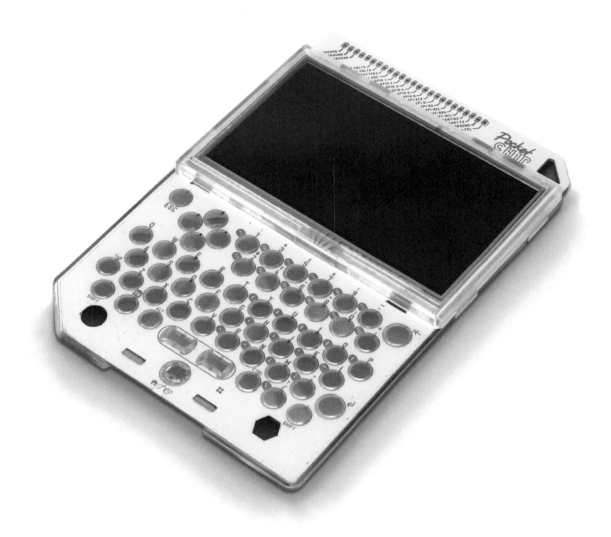

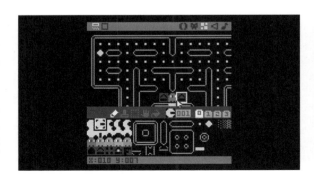

072.

Pokémon Gashapon toy

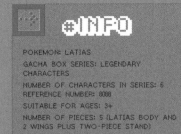

#INFO

POKÉMON: LATIAS
GACHA BOX SERIES: LEGENDARY CHARACTERS
NUMBER OF CHARACTERS IN SERIES: 6
REFERENCE NUMBER: 8088
SUITABLE FOR AGES: 3+
NUMBER OF PIECES: 5 (LATIAS BODY AND 2 WINGS PLUS TWO-PIECE STAND)

As any Pokémon aficionado will know, Latias is a 'Legendary Pokémon' whose special powers include the ability to levitate, learn human speech, and 'Sight Share' with her male counterpart Latios. Appearing in a number of Nintendo's wildly successful Pokémon videogames, Latias has also played a starring role on the big screen in the 'Pokémon Heroes' animé.

Here, Latias is shown in the form of a small, plastic toy supplied in a capsule obtained from the kind of coin-operated 'lucky dip' vending machine that continues to grace the foyers of supermarkets and grocery stores all over the world. In Japan, department stores dedicate large areas of prime retail floor space to the machines, which are lined up in rows almost as far as the eye can see and stacked two or three machines high.

Insert a coin, twist the handle, and out pops a hollow, opaque plastic ball. Sealed around the seam with branding and safety information, the ball (or 'box' as they are often called) contains and conceals the mystery prize within. Only when broken open does the capsule reveal its contents.

Capsule toys are almost always made available in themed sets, usually oriented around a specific licence such as Pokémon, with one toy from the range delivered per capsule. The randomness of the coin-operated delivery mechanism ensures that in the tradition of collectible football stickers or, indeed, packs of Pokémon cards, one never knows exactly what one is going to get, or whether one's collection will ever be completed. These capsule toys are often collectively referred to 'Gashapon' though this is, in fact, the brand name of Bandai's particular series of vending machine offerings. This Pokémon example comes from Tomy's 'Gacha Box' range, and is one of six models in the 'Legendary Pokémon' series produced in 2009.

Of course, collecting would be no fun – or at least would present little challenge – without scarcity. Just as in the videogame, the Gacha Box retail system has its own built-in frustration mechanisms that create and manage scarcity. Not only are the contents of the individual boxes unknowable pre-purchase and delivered by the seemingly arbitrary twist of a lever, but also not all figures are necessarily equally commonly distributed in the boxes, and collections are not universally available worldwide. Tomy's online commentary on the 'Legendary Pokémon' set reminds us of its rarity. 'As this box was not released in all countries, these buildable figures are very rare and sought after by Pokémon collectors.'

In the videogame, acquiring rare Pokémon without the prescribed effort (or luck) is virtually impossible, at least without cheating, as the game code and its pseudo-random algorithms hold the key. Unless you can make a sneaky trade with some poor dupe who doesn't know what they've got hold of. By contrast, collectors of Gacha Box toys can more easily (if not more cheaply) work around the limitations of artificial scarcity and differentiated territorial releases by turning to specialist retailers, or to eBay, to purchase specific figures and finally Catch 'Em All.

▲ Above: Unopened Pokémon 'Gacha Box'.

▶ Right: Assembled Pokémon Gashapon toy.

073.
Pokémon Master Trainer board game
1999

Even though it's been over 20 years since Pikachu, Squirtle, Charmander and friends first appeared, it's still hard to pin down exactly what Pokémon is (or perhaps, are?) There are 721 distinct species of them in the wild at the moment. They've been seen on collectible cards, T-shirts, lunchboxes, board games, the nose cones of Jumbo Jets, and even freely roaming around the streets waiting to be caught by Pokémon Go trainers... You see, Pokémon isn't really anything. Pokémon is everything.

Pokémon is the brainchild of Japanese videogame developer Satoshi Tajiri. As a child, Tajiri was fascinated by collecting insects and tadpoles – such was his interest that his friends nicknamed him 'Dr Bug' – and it was the desire to share this passion with a new generation of children that led to the concepts at the heart of Pokémon. In 1996, after six years in development, the game was released for the Nintendo Game Boy and the world began to memorize the names of 151 new creatures, each possessing their own unique powers, capabilities and weaknesses. Over time, Pokémon would go on to become the second bestselling videogame series ever – pipped only by Nintendo's own Super Mario series.

Part of the genius of Pokémon comes from its combination of imaginative character designs, lavishly produced artwork picturing each creature and their habitat in minute detail, and the complex patterns of evolution that link the different creatures together, requiring prolonged play to unlock their full potential. Pikachu, the loveable electric mouse becomes Raichu, sleepy Jigglypuff eventually transforms into Wigglytuff, and Koffing becomes Weezing. And, as the game's slogan says, to be the best you 'Gotta Catch 'em all!'.

Luckily, for those unable to be able to catch that one elusive creature, there is another option: trading. In the collectible card game, this is straightforward, even if the negotiations might be complex – just how many Rattatas is a holographic Meowth worth? In the videogame, trading is ingenious. Making use of the Game Boy's Link Cable accessory, even the first Japanese release of Pokémon actually consisted of two separate games: Pokémon Red and Green (these would become Red and Blue outside Japan). Although the two games were basically the same, there were some crucial differences, and neither Red nor Green contained all 151 Pokémon. To 'Catch 'em All!', you either needed to

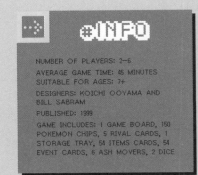

NUMBER OF PLAYERS: 2–6

AVERAGE GAME TIME: 45 MINUTES
SUITABLE FOR AGES: 7+

DESIGNERS: KOICHI OOYAMA AND
BILL SABRAM

PUBLISHED: 1999

GAME INCLUDES: 1 GAME BOARD, 150
POKEMON CHIPS, 5 RIVAL CARDS, 1
STORAGE TRAY, 54 ITEMS CARDS, 54
EVENT CARDS, 6 ASH MOVERS, 2 DICE

trade with a friend who had the other game – or to buy both, and a second Game Boy to go with them.

And so the scene was set. Pokémon wasn't a videogame. It was at least two videogames. In 1999, it also became a board game... Released by Hasbro and Milton Bradley, Pokémon Master Trainer is based on the first generation of Pokémon (although Mew is not included) and features characters and locations from the original videogame and TV series. With cardboard chips representing the different pocket monsters, between 2–6 players (ages 7 and up) each assume the role of Ash Ketchum (represented in glorious plastic) travelling across the Kanto region to reach Indigo Plateau for the final battle against one of the Elite Four.

▲ Above: Pokemon Master Trainer Board
game retail packaging (top); detail of board and
accessories (bottom).

Prepaid purchase cards

ITUNES CARD DENOMINATIONS: £25, £50, £100
APPLE APP STORE LAUNCHED: 10 JULY 2008
NINTENDO ESHOP CARD DENOMINATIONS UK: £25
(MARIO AND LUIGI), £50 (DONKEY KONG AND DK JR),
£100 (BOWSER)
NINTENDO ESHOP CARD DENOMINATIONS US: $10
(BOWSER), $20 (MARIO AND LUIGI), $35 (LUIGI),
$50 (MARIO)
NINTENDO ESHOP LAUNCHED: 6 JUNE 2011 (3DS),
18 NOVEMBER 2012 (WII U), 3 MARCH 2017 (SWITCH)

The history of videogames is the history of storage media. From 5.25 inch floppy disks, through 3.5 inch floppy disks, to tape cassettes, cartridges, cards, CDs, DVDs, Blu-Rays, and more, there is an almost bewildering array of different formats. And that's before we even get to the different types of cartridges or the inherent incompatibilities between different cartridges or discs designed for different platforms. Yet, for all their differences, one thing each of these storage media have in common is that they have a physical, material presence. They are things. They are things that you can touch, share with friends, and collect. They're also things that can get damaged, broken, and lost (because your friends never gave them back).

One trend in videogaming in the early 21st century has been the shift towards the digital distribution of videogames. Rather than a disc or a cartridge, we have a download. It's all still data, but when we download it from a server or an online store, we never get to hold a physical object in our hand. The data resides on our machine, our console, or our handheld, and not on a disc or cartridge.

This isn't a situation unique to videogames. The shift towards digital distribution has also profoundly affected the way we purchase, watch and listen to music, film and television. And, as we download – or, increasingly, stream – film, television and music content, sales of physical media like CDs and DVDs decline.

Even a cursory look at the current console and handheld marketplace will tell us that physical media haven't disappeared. PlayStation 4, Xbox One, Switch, and 3DS all have optical disc or cartridge slots. But all also have online stores for digitally downloading games, demos, and updates. If we look at the world of smartphone gaming, the picture is rather different, with the Apple App Store and Google Play Store becoming the hubs for the distribution and discovery of gaming experiences. And then there's Steam for the PC and Mac gamer.

With the coming of the online store and the digital download, the act of buying games has shifted, too. Make an account, link a payment card, and you can be playing Stardew Valley, Minecraft or Ark: Survival Evolved in just a few moments (broadband speeds permitting). We can't yet say that the era of purchasing physical discs or cartridges with notes and coins is gone, but it is increasingly common for a digital download to be purchased with a secure digital payment. Not many decades ago, when the first cartridges were being set out on shelves in department stores, this level of virtuality would have seemed like science fiction.

But for those not wishing to shop online today or wanting to gift a game, there remains an analogue solution even in the world of digital downloads. By travelling to a bricks-and-mortar store, you can purchase a pre-paid card. By means of a unique serial number revealed by removing the scratch-off panel, the card's recipient can credit your cash to an account, and the downloading can begin.

The prepaid card has been a real area of growth within the retail sector, and shoppers will recognize the expanding space that stores and supermarkets dedicate to rows upon rows of Steam, App Store, Play Store, PlayStation Network, Xbox, and Nintendo eStore cards... to name but a few!

▶ Right: Apple prepaid card (top);
Nintendo eStore prepaid card (bottom).

075.

Quickshot
Joystick

1982

Long before we touched screens, mashed gamepads or even moved mice, the dominant input method for many videogames was the joystick. Originally developed for use in aviation, this versatile stick control found a natural home in videogames, its robust design making it the perfect input mechanism for the wear and tear it would suffer in the arcades of the seventies.

With the advent of home computers, players demanded an experience as close as possible to that of the arcades. Even if the sound and graphics on their 48k Spectrum weren't quite as immersive as the commercial stand-up machines, the feel of a real joystick in your hand made up for a lot. Home computers needed joysticks. Joysticks needed to become add-on peripherals.

The sudden popularity of the Atari 2600 home console placed the joystick that it was supplied with, the CX40, into the hands of millions. Such was the impact of that controller's design that it survives as a key icon of videogames to this day. Despite being wildly popular, however, the CX40 developed a reputation for being a difficult device to use. Cramp-

inducingly hard to hold in the hand, the sticks would usually meet the end of their life when their fragile internal workings were broken through an excess of force, applied by an excitable gamer. Through the popularity of the CX40 though, Atari established a standard for joystick controller ports. Making its first non-Atari appearance on the VIC-20 in 1981, the 'Atari Joystick port' opened up the market to peripheral manufacturers.

The Quickshot series of controllers was introduced by Spectravideo in the early 1980s, and attempted to address a number of the problems with the CX40 and its clones. The addition of rubber suction cups on the base removed the need for the stick to be held in the hand. When secured to a table, the Quickshot could be comfortably used, as long as the player wasn't too enthusiastic. The stick also introduced an ergonomic design, building contours for the grip which hugely enhanced the feel of the controller over the Atari original.

The Quickshot II, released in 1983, was one of the most popular designs in the series. As well as moving both of the two buttons onto the stick (one as a trigger), the designers also

acknowledged the popularity of 'shoot-em-up' games at the time. Onto the base of the joystick a new switch was added, 'auto-fire'. When turned on, it would simulate repeated rapid presses of the fire button – dispensing relentless projectiles towards whatever villain the player was facing in game and saving their trigger finger from cramp.

The Quickshot series of joysticks was priced low, relatively robust (excepting when tested by 'Decathlon' style games) and enjoyed remarkable popularity throughout the early home-computing years.

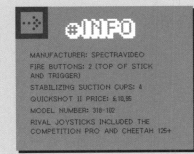

#INFO

MANUFACTURER: SPECTRAVIDEO
FIRE BUTTONS: 2 (TOP OF STICK AND TRIGGER)
STABILIZING SUCTION CUPS: 4
QUICKSHOT II PRICE: £10.95
MODEL NUMBER: 318-102
RIVAL JOYSTICKS INCLUDED THE COMPETITION PRO AND CHEETAH 125+

▶ Right: Quickshot Joystick unit.

076.

R4i cartridge (counterfeit)

2010

●INFO

CART COMPATIBLE WITH: DS, DSI, DS LITE
SUPPLIED WITH: MICRO SD CARD, USB ADAPTER
FEATURES INCLUDE: DLDI AUTOPATCHING;
SUPPORT FOR MOONSHELL AND OTHER
HOMEBREW; SDHC CARDS UP TO 32GB
MADE IN: CHINA

The Revolution for DS (more commonly known at the 'R4') looks like a standard Nintendo DS game cartridge and, to some extent, behaves like a standard Nintendo DS cartridge. Why, then, were Nintendo so determined to see it banned?

The short answer is that the R4 allows backups of commercial games to be executed on the handheld console. That sounds really handy. After all, who doesn't want to backup their games just in case you lose your original cartridge or the dog eats it?

Better still, by removing the micro SD card from the slot in the side of the R4 and attaching it to a computer, hundreds of backups could be stored and accessed from a single cart. Booting the R4, the player can choose the game they want to play from the list in custom interface. Once selected, the game boots just as it would as if it was running on the original DS cartridge. It really is as simple as that. Say goodbye to cumbersome carrying cases of DS carts or those tricky decisions about which games to take with you on that trip and which to leave at home - which you almost immediately regretted once you'd arrived. Just load them up and onto a single R4 and take them all.

So, what didn't Nintendo like about it? Was it eating into their DS cartridge case market? Perhaps, but that wasn't the real issue. The real issue was 'making a backup' sounds like a perfectly reasonable thing to do. You buy a game and backup the data just in case something happens to the original. However, from Nintendo's perspective, what the R4 was really about was allowing people to download and share 'backups' that they had never bought and that they had no intention of purchasing. For Nintendo, this was about software piracy and the R4's ability to store and run 'backups' was another way of describing storing and running illegally ripped games. To be clear, the R4 doesn't enable ripping of the game itself, just the storage and execution of the code. But, with the whole of the Internet at their disposal, finding backups of even brand new games proved to be not too difficult for those suitably determined.

Pursuing the R4's makers as well as seeking to restrict the sale and advertising of the devices, Nintendo claimed that the carts were enabling piracy and that their means of working illegally bypassed its proprietary security systems.

As part of its anti-piracy campaign, Nintendo claimed that consumers were harmed by inferior, counterfeit products and also that piracy undermined the work and threatened the livelihoods of the teams of game developers legitimately making games for its systems.

Courts in the UK, France, Germany, Australia and Japan are among those to have declared the R4 flashcart illegal. Nonetheless, and now made by a different manufacturer, similar cards bearing an altogether similar name remain available online for use with the DS and 3DS systems.

Ironically, the popularity of R4 carts was such that they were counterfeited with fake versions widely available in 2010. The images here are of a counterfeit 'R4i Ultra' card and packaging.

▲ Above: (clockwise from top left) Nintendo DS, stylus, R4i unit with micro SD card and USB adapter.

▶ Right: R4i unit front and rear (counterfeit).

RetroPie
portable console
2017

COMPATIBLE WITH: RASPBERRY PI A, A+, B, B+, 2, ZERO AND 3)

MINIMUM SD CARD CAPACITY FOR RETROPIE 4,3 RPI3 BUILD: 8GB

SYSTEMS EMULATED: 54 FROM 3DO TO ZX SPECTRUM

PORTS: ADVENTURE GAME STUDIO, DOOM, MARATHON, MINECRAFT, QUAKE

CONTROLLER COMPATIBILITY: WII REMOTE, XBOX 360 GAMEPAD, PS4, WII U PRO CONTROLLER

UNDER THE HOOD: RETROARCH AND LIBRETRO API

You might be able to work out what RetroPie is by looking at its name. It's a retrogaming application that runs on the Raspberry Pi. That all seems pretty straightforward, and it's not a bad name for the software. But such a simple description belies the extraordinary technical achievement that RetroPie represents and the range of uses to which it can be put.

At its heart, RetroPie is an emulation tool. It isn't an emulator in itself, but rather an application that gathers together, keeps updated, and hosts emulators for a whole range of different gaming devices and platforms.

Let's back up a bit, what exactly is an emulator? Without getting into the minute details of coding and circuit modelling, an emulator is a piece of software that allows one hardware system to mimic the behaviour of another. The upshot is that by running a videogame emulator, you can turn a general purpose computer into a Nintendo 64, a Commodore Amiga 1200, an Atari 2600... Emulators run on all sorts of systems for all kinds of reasons. You can run them on a PC or a Macintosh to emulate systems from the 1980s, 1990s and 2000s. In fact, the retro games that you can buy on the Nintendo eStore or download to your phone as part of Sega Forever all run on emulators. To be able to turn your phone into a Sega Mega Drive is a pretty remarkable feat.

Remarkable perhaps, but even entry-level PCs, Macs and smartphones are pretty expensive machines so, if we overlook the fact that emulation seems like a combination of coding and magic, we might hope that they could run processor- and graphics-intensive applications. It's far from easy to produce emulators, of course, but it's worth remembering that a modern smartphone is many times more powerful than a 1990s gaming system, which definitely helps.

So, what's so special about RetroPie? As well as being a one-stop-shop that manages attached controllers and provides a beautiful and customizable interface complete with info and cover art for all your games, RetroPie runs on the Raspberry Pi, and that's what makes it special. The top of the range Raspberry Pi 3 retails for £35 in the UK, and RetroPie will actually run on the cut-down Pi zero which will set you back about £6. You don't get much of a PC or Mac for that. Presumably, the RetroPie software is expensive though? You might think

so given that it effectively provides access to more than 50 retrogaming consoles, computers and arcade systems, including comparative rarities like the Nintendo Virtual Boy, Sega 32X and Dragon 32. If you wanted to buy the original hardware, you'd be looking at parting with some serious cash. That makes RetroPie's price tag of completely free even more enticing! Download it, write it to an SD card, boot the PI, plug in a USB keyboard or joypad and you're good to go...

Well nearly. What to play? That's where things get a little tricky because, although you have all the systems at your disposal, getting access to the commercially available games – or 'ROMs' as they are called in the emulation community – usually involves ripping data from cartridges, CDs or DVDs. This involves circumventing copy protection, which is almost invariably against the law. As such, RetroPie isn't distributed with any copyrighted games – not quite the same as saying nobody that downloads it plays copyrighted games with it, of course.

▶ Right: RetroPie software running Sonic the Hedgehog (with SNES-style controller).

Scent of
Success
2009

Videogame trade shows have, for years, been characterized by the presence of the promotional item. Over the years attendees have accumulated sackfuls of branded goods, some good, most not, but all doing their part to raise awareness of their product and keep landfill sites full. If you're working on a game with strong characters and iconography, producing these items is a reasonably easy task (elsewhere in this book, you can read about the promotional 'Ocarina of Time'), but if your game is more symbolic...

Football Manager is a sales juggernaut, but not an obvious candidate for merchandising. Widely regarded as a gamified spreadsheet, once all the promotional footballs and squad shirts have been made, it's hard to know where to go next. In 2009, Sports Interactive, developers of the game, hatched a plan to try and get more coverage in the mainstream media. Specifically, on national television.

The conceit was to capture the delicate pheromones emitted by a football team after they won a match, synthesize them into a fragrance, and produce an aspirational deodorant for men. In victorious changing rooms after matches, Sports Interactive scientists claimed to 'capture' the stench of victory. They released it as

the 'scent of success', with a deodorant manufacturer partner.

The idea certainly captured the imagination of the lifestyle news cycle, and even made it as far as being discussed on morning television magazine programmes. Videogames are seldom discussed on mainstream media apart from outcries about violence or celebrations of blockbuster releases. 'The scent of success' brought some welcome wit into videogame marketing even if it did, as a senior Sports Interactive executive commented, "smell awful".

MADE BY: SPORTS INTERACTIVE
GIVEN AWAY WITH: FOOTBALL MANAGER 2009
COMBINES: GRASS, SWEAT, BOOT LEATHER AND HEAT SPRAY
ACCORDING TO MILES JACOBSON OF SPORTS INTERACTIVE, "OUR SCENT WILL BRING THE DRESSING ROOM INTO THE HOMES OF FOOTBALL MANAGER 2009 PLAYERS, INSPIRING THEM FOR PRE-MATCH TEAM TALKS, PREPARING THEM TO DIRECT THEIR TEAM FROM THE SIDELINES AND PRIME THEM FOR A TRICKY PRESS CONFERENCE."

▲ Above: Football Manager 2007 promotional drinks mats and box.

▶ Right: 'Scent of Success' body spray.

Release the scent of a winning team's dressing room

© Sports Interactive 2008

Sega Game Gear
TV Tuner

1992

TV STANDARD: NTSC OR PAL DEPENDING ON REGION
TUNER TYPE: ANALOGUE
SYSTEM BATTERY LIFE: VERY LIMITED
AERIAL: TELESCOPIC
VIDEO INPUT: YES
ORIGINAL PRICE: £74.99 (UK)
BANDS: UHF AND VHF

When is a game console not a game console? When it's a TV!

But surely, videogame consoles exist to stop you watching TV – because TV is so last century – so non-interactive? However, just as a handheld console lets you take your gaming with you, imagine if you could take your TV as well. Imagine being able to play or watch on the move. Anywhere. Any time. For anything up to a couple of hours before the batteries ran out (sorry to spoil it, but the batteries really didn't last very long in this thing).

This adapter turns the Sega Game Gear into a fully-fledged portable television. Now, in a word of tablets, phones, Hulu and the BBC iPlayer, this might not sound like a big deal, but in the 1990s, handheld portable TVs were comparatively rare and absolutely pricey.

The Game Gear TV Tuner is actually a surprisingly versatile device. It plugs into the console's cartridge slot and allows full colour analogue TV to be viewed on the handheld's display. There's good and bad news there. The good news is that it reminds us how technologically advanced the Game Gear is. Compared with other handheld videogame

consoles, which had pretty small and decidedly greenish-grey displays (ahem, Game Boy, we're looking at you), Sega were keen to promote the TV Tuner as it showcased the Game Gear's large, colourful screen. That was also the reason it got through batteries like they were going out of fashion – which was the bad news.

The extra bad news for anybody wanting to use a Game Gear Tuner today is that it only picks up analogue TV signals so, as the world shifts inexorably towards digital broadcasting, the Game Gear Tuner becomes capable of displaying little more than static and interference, which can get pretty boring after a

while. However, there is a solution, because built into the TV Tuner is an AV input. This means that you can plug in a camcorder or a VCR and watch all your favourite VHS or Betamax tapes on the Game Gear screen. Old school.

Just make sure you have a really long extension cable for the VCR and plenty of batteries for the Game Gear if you want to see the end of your favourite programme.

▲ Above: SEGA Game Gear unit.

▶ Right: Game Gear TV Tuner (PAL version).

SID
Chip
1983

The Sound Interface Device, or SID chip as it is more commonly known, is the sound chip at the heart of the 1982 Commodore 64 home computer. It is responsible for creating all the jumping and blasting sound effects and every single note of musical accompaniment to the thousands of games that were released for the system. So, whether it's well-loved tunes like Rob Hubbard's Commando, Martin Galway's Wizball, or Chris Huelsbeck's Turrican, all the bass lines, drum tracks, and screaming guitar solos are generated by the SID chip.

Given that it had to handle every sonic element for every game, it's surprising to learn just how limited the capabilities of the SID chip seem to be. It can play just three notes at once. Imagine a guitar with three strings, or playing the piano but only being able to use three fingers. By comparison, the sound chip in the Nintendo Entertainment System could play five notes simultaneously, while arcade machines often used multiple sound chips combined with speech synthesizers to create their sounds. But the SID plays just three. Oh, and all the music has to be programmed in assembly language. No musical notation, just code representing each note, instrument and drum.

However, in other ways, the SID is an incredibly powerful device with sound-shaping capabilities unmatched by anything else available at the time in a home computer, console or coin-op. This might have something to do with the fact that the SID chip was designed by an engineer named Bob Yannes. As well as being a skilled chip designer, Bob was a musician. Unimpressed with the quality of sound chips and with aspirations to create a chip that could power the kinds of musical instruments you might see on stage or in the recording studio, he set about creating something that would blow everything else out of the water. And he succeeded. And after leaving Commodore, he went on to found a company called Ensoniq, whose synthesizers and samplers revolutionized the musical instrument business.

So, it's a sophisticated synthesizer, but how did all those incredible tunes come out of just three notes? Well, that's where the magic of composers like Hubbard, Galway and Huelsbeck come in. Skilled programmers as well as talented musicians, they developed a host of tricks to fool the ear into hearing more than three notes at once. For example, listen to almost any piece of Commodore 64 music and you hear warbling chords that sound a bit like a mobile phone ringtone. That's a classic SID chip technique. If a pattern of two or three notes are played in quick succession

DESIGNED BY: ROBERT 'BOB' YANNES
MANUFACTURED BY: MOS TECHNOLOGY
VARIANTS: 6581 AND 8580
OSCILLATORS: THREE WITH VARIABLE WAVEFORMS AND 8 OCTAVE PITCH RANGE, VOLUME ENVELOPE PER OSCILLATOR, RING MODULATION, PULSE WIDTH MODULATION FILTER: MULTI MODE WITH RESONANCE THE SID CHIP ALSO HAS TWO 8-BIT CONVERTERS FOR GAME CONTROL PADDLE/MOUSE INPUT

(really quick succession – faster than any player could play by hand) we stop hearing them as separate notes and hear a chord – a warbling one, perhaps, but a chord nonetheless. So, out of just one note comes three!

The characteristic sounds of these 1980s composers mean that their music is as loved today as ever, with concerts celebrating their work held all over the world. And the SID chip's raw, gritty sound is equally prized by electronic musicians, whose chiptune desires are catered for by modern musical instrument manufacturers producing software that emulates its sound, or even building keyboards with real SID chips built in. So, Bob Yannes got his wish in the end, and the SID chip is now the heart of synthesizers on stage and in studios around the word!

▲ Above: MOS Technologies 6581 'SID' chip
(manufactured in the 23rd week of 1983).

Sinclair ZX Spectrum 48K

1982

#INFO

DEVELOPMENT CODENAME: ZX82
OPERATING SYSTEM: SINCLAIR BASIC
PROCESSOR: ZILOG Z80 AT 3.5MHZ
PLACE OF MANUFACTURE: DUNDEE, SCOTLAND (AT THE OLD TIMEX FACTORY)
KEYBOARD FEEL: RUBBERY

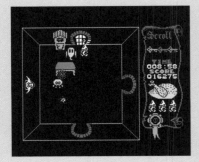

While the BBC was delivering the Rolls Royce of home computers – pricey but produced with the highest quality components and sold as a trusted device into British schools – Clive Sinclair took a different tack. When the school kids of the UK went home at the end of the day, few of them could afford a BBC Micro at home on which to continue their adventures. Spotting the insatiable appetite for home computers that was rapidly developing in the early 1980s, Sinclair set about producing the most affordable computer possible.

His first machines, the ZX80 and ZX81, met with some success in this burgeoning market. But it was the ZX Spectrum (so named because it delivered colour graphics) that really cemented his place in the history of videogames. The ZX Spectrum (Speccy, to those who loved it) was a budget computer, intended for as many people as possible. The product design, created by newly graduated designer Rick Dickinson, introduced a remarkable budget-saving innovation in the form of the 'membrane' keyboard. The rubbery keys, formed of one single sheet inside the casing, proved to be the signature component in the device.

This wasn't the computer that was in schools, it was the computer that people came home to. As a result of its accessibility, it became the entry point for a generation of videogame makers. As bedrooms were repurposed into development studios, the UK games industry of today was effectively born in a few years of white-hot productivity. The Oliver Twins, the Stamper twins, and David Perry all enjoyed early success on the platform, learning their trade and establishing the foundations for lifelong careers.

Perhaps more than anything else, the ZX Spectrum was defined by its relationship with its bitter rival, the Commodore 64. A vicious marketing war broke out between the two machines and whilst both were affordable, few families would invest in both. "Commodore or Spectrum?" was an often-heard line of questioning in playgrounds around the UK. Choose your side.

Both platforms ultimately declined commercially, but they retain special, permanent places in the gaming consciousness, as evidenced by the recent trend in playable hardware tributes.

▲ Above: Favourite Spectrum games included Horace Goes Skiing (left and centre) and Atic Atac (right).

▶ Right: The ZX Spectrum 48K with its characteristic rainbow flash.

•INFO

MANUFACTURER: SNK
AVAILABILITY: 1999–2000 (1999–2001 IN JAPAN)
INITIAL PRICE: $69.95
PROCESSOR: TOSHIBA TLCS900H RUNNING AT 6.144MHZ
AND ZILOG Z80 RUNNING AT 3.072MHZ
DISPLAY SIZE: 2.7 INCHES (NOT BACKLIT)
DISPLAY RESOLUTION: 160 X 152 PIXELS
POWER REQUIREMENTS: 2 X AA BATTERIES (ESTIMATED
40 HOURS PLAY TIME); CR2032 FOR CLOCK AND
MEMORY BACKUP
REGION LOCKOUT: NONE

Ah, the Neo Geo. Just the name is enough to make gamers of a certain age dewy-eyed. SNK's console was just so big, so impressive, so... expensive. With cartridges the size of other consoles and which cost hundreds of pounds, this was the luxury end of the market. If you liked arcade conversions, there was nothing wrong with the Mega Drive, SNES or Jaguar (well, maybe the Jaguar could have had a slightly better library of games), but the Neo Geo was an arcade machine. This wasn't about conversions. This was an arcade system, and those gigantic cartridges were basically the same boards that plugged into the coin-op cabinets.

So, when SNK announced the Neo Geo Pocket, hopes were high. It's difficult to imagine how exciting it would be to have SNK's technology on the move. However, where the Neo Geo home console (known as the AES or Advanced Entertainment System) was all about ultra high-power and arcade quality entertainment, the Neo Geo Pocket was an altogether more modest device. Modest and even, dare we say it, a little bit disappointing. OK, so it was unrealistic to expect arcade-perfect mobile

versions of King of Fighters but, with the Game Boy and Game Boy Color dominating the marketplace, and with devices like Atari's Lynx and Sega's Game Gear all having colour displays, the original 1998 Neo Geo Pocket's monochrome screen looked rather lacklustre. In fact, low sales of the Pocket meant that it was not released outside Asia.

So, that was the end of that? Another handheld that didn't manage to topple Nintendo's Game Boy? Not quite. A year after the original black and white Pocket, SNK launched the Neo Geo Pocket Color. And guess what? It had a colour display.

And it's battery life was pretty impressive. Forty hours from a single set of AAs was many times better than Game Gear or Lynx owners could expect. Systems could be linked together for multiplayer gaming, and there were some good titles, including conversions of popular arcade fighters in the King of Fighters and SNK vs Capcom series. Sega even brought their spiky blue mascot to the system with Sonic the Hedgehog Pocket Adventure. The link-up with Sega even extended to being able to connect the Neo Geo Pocket Color to the Dreamcast.

And yet, after a promising start, it all started to slow down. Despite innovations like the link cables and the joystick that took the place of the more common D-Pad, SNK never really got the marketing message right. But what really did it for the Neo Geo Pocket Color were the Pocket Monsters. The popularity of Pokémon ensured that Game Boy continued to rule the roost, and by 2001 SNK had gone out of business. Gone but not forgotten, the Neo Geo Pocket Color remains popular among collectors and there's no denying that the Neo Geo name tugs at the heartstrings.

▲ Above: UK retail packaging.

▶ Right: SNK Neo Geo Pocket Color unit (blue version).

Sony
PlayStation 4

2013

With the launch of the Playstation in 1994, Sony suddenly, swiftly reinvented what a home videogame console could be if it was part of our lifestyle. Elevated from being a niche pastime for boys, the Playstation delivered an urgent, carefully constructed cool with a global brand and razor-sharp marketing.

The Playstation 2 reinforced and expanded the project. Arriving at precisely the right moment as VHS cassettes were dying, the PS2 invited us to not just play our games, but also our shiny new DVD movies on it. It showed us how it could be at the epicentre of our digital lives with ease. It was all going so well when the Playstation 3 stalled. Developers found the new system incredibly difficult to work on, leading to a dearth of anticipated launch titles, and the console was plagued with compatibility issues surrounding PS2 titles that people had already bought. Nintendo, with their playfully inventive Wii, and Microsoft with the X-box 360 had already stolen their dominance by the time PS3 hit the shops. It didn't help that the PS3 was also very expensive.

Amended versions of the console managed to claw back some commercial success, but Sony were now in the unfamiliar position of playing catch-up. As time passed, gaming started to be transformed by the emergence of YouTube, Twitch and social media. People started to share their performances in games, extending the visibility of 'playing' far beyond the moment when they are sitting at home actually doing so.

The Playstation 4, announced in 2013, was a refocusing on Sony's pledge to the purity of playing. Gone were the claims of being a home-media hub – as the marketing line put it, this was "for the players." Inside the box, the hardware architecture was essentially a high-powered PC, suddenly making it much easier (and cheaper) for developers to work on. These radically lowered costs also made the platform a viable place for independent developers to work on too, bringing along a rash of indie-credibility to the system.

Other than raw gaming power, PS4's defining focus at launch was about social play. It invited players to stream their game-play live through

services they already used, share screenshots of moments they wanted to celebrate and capture game-play for editing later. They even provided the editing software. Such was the commitment to its social focus that the new dual shock controller – still based around the core design from the PS1 – deftly made it physical. Alongside the iconic Playstation symbols and a neat new touchpad sat a new button that encapsulated where gaming had progressed to. It was labelled with a single word: 'share'.

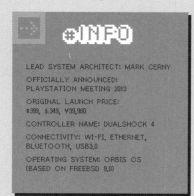

#INFO

LEAD SYSTEM ARCHITECT: MARK CERNY

OFFICIALLY ANNOUNCED: PLAYSTATION MEETING 2013

ORIGINAL LAUNCH PRICE: $399, £349, ¥39,980

CONTROLLER NAME: DUALSHOCK 4

CONNECTIVITY: WI-FI, ETHERNET, BLUETOOTH, USB3.0

OPERATING SYSTEM: ORBIS OS (BASED ON FREEBSD 9.0)

▶ Right: PlayStation 4 console and Dual Shock controller.

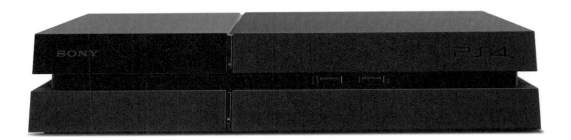

Space Invaders
Arcade Cabinet

1978

#INFO

DESIGNED BY:
TOMOHIRO NISHIKADO

MANUFACTURED BY:
TAITO (JAPAN)
AND BALLY (US)

CPU: INTEL 8080 AT 2MHZ;

CABINET STYLE:
ORIGINALLY COCKTAIL
STYLE THEN UPRIGHT

NUMBER OF MONSTERS ON CABINET: 7

It wasn't the first arcade game. It wasn't even the first shooting game. But, in 1978, Taito's Space Invaders was the biggest game in town. In fact, the game was so popular in its home country of Japan that it reputedly caused a shortage of 100 Yen coins, because so many had been put inside the machines, and they couldn't be retrieved quickly enough!

And it wasn't just Japan. Space Invaders was the first globally successful videogame. There had been popular videogames before, but Space Invaders was different. It was a cultural icon and its fame spread across the world like wildfire – like an invasion.

Space Invaders was created by Tomohiro Nishikado, who had been inspired by games such as Atari's brick-busting Breakout. Comparing the two, the similarities are clear, with the player's bat becoming a spaceship that can still only move left and right and the wall of bricks evolving into aliens. Swap the bouncing ball for a missile and the transformation is complete. Well, almost. In Breakout, the bricks don't move, but in Space Invaders, the waves of aliens not only march left and right as they try to evade the player's fire, they also descend down the screen. As they inch ever closer to Earth, they get faster and faster (fun fact: they get faster after each alien is destroyed because the

system has to draw fewer objects on screen). Dispatch them all, and a new wave appears. And so it goes on. For ever and ever. Until you lose. And, like many games of the so-called 'Golden Era' you *will* lose, either because you run out of ships or run out of patience and walk away from the machine mid-game. The invasion is inevitable and all you can do is try to postpone it for as long as humanly possible.

Such was the game's popularity, that countless home versions were created, and it became one of the earliest 'killer apps'. A killer app is a piece of software so desirable that people will buy the hardware it runs on just to be able to use it (think Game Boy and Tetris or Xbox and Halo).

Decades later, those little aliens are among the most recognizable videogame characters. Yet, however immediately recognizable they might still be, have you ever stopped to think what those relentless invading aliens actually are? Well, according to Nishikado, they're octopuses, squid and crabs. Space crabs? Yes, that's right. The 'space' part comes from George Lucas' *Star Wars*, which, since its release in 1977, had given rise to a host of interstellar films and TV programmes, while the 'crabs' are a reference to H.G. Wells' *War of the Worlds* – which also partly inspired the alien invasion theme. Space crabs – it

all makes sense now. Maybe that's why they only move sideways? Maybe.

So, like many truly innovative designs, Space Invaders can trace its origins to a number of quite specific references from literature, film and other videogames. One other surprising area of innovation was the way in which the original coin-operated Space Invaders machine achieved its colour graphics. Everything on screen is actually drawn in black and white, but by the magic of multicoloured transparent strips of film stuck on the TV screen, the aliens turn red, blue and yellow. Just like real space crabs.

▲ Above: Stand-up cabinet
showing Space Invaders artwork.

◀ Left: Space Invaders' graphics were
reflected onto a painted backdrop.

Spaceteam
Admiral's Club Medal

#INFO

SPACETEAM RELEASED: 1 NOVEMBER 2012
DEVELOPER: HENRY SMITH, SLEEPING
BEAST GAMES
GENRE: CO-OPERATIVE SHOUTING GAME
SPACETEAM DOWNLOADS: 4 MILLION
SPACETEAM VARIATIONS: SPACETEAM ESL
(ENGLISH AS A SECOND LANGUAGE);
SPACETEAM CARD GAME (3-6 PLAYERS)

'Do you like pushing buttons and shouting at your friends? Do you like discharging Clip-jawed Fluxtrunions? If you answered yes, or no, then you might have what it takes to be on a Spaceteam!'

If the opening lines of the official description of the game tell you one thing, it's that Spaceteam is silly. Gloriously silly. Unashamedly silly. Developed and published by Henry Smith and released for the iOS and Android platforms in 2012, it is the first and perhaps still the only title in the 'multiplayer co-operative shouting game' genre.

The premise of the game is pretty simple. You and the rest of your Spaceteam pilot a spaceship. Unsurprisingly, the Spaceteam has to stop the ship from crashing. More surprisingly, not crashing the spaceship is the object of the game. It's not about stopping it crashing in order to fly off and discover new planets, battle invading aliens, or make cargo deliveries to faraway systems; you just stop it crashing for as long as possible.

Each player is put in charge of a random control panel which is shown on the screen of their smartphone or tablet. Each control panel has a number of dials, switches, sliders and buttons, each labelled with absurd

technobabble like Vent Core, Hyperjig and Spectrobolt. As the game begins, players receive instructions on their screens with orders required to keep the spaceship flying. These orders also come in the form of nonsense. 'Engage Stringorb', 'Flood Synchronous Z-Loop', 'Increase Artificial Grill to 3'. Importantly, because they don't know who has the Artificial Grill control, the orders have to be communicated to the other members of the Spaceteam which means players have to say out loud this techno-piffle. This leads to laughing and, as the game speeds up, shouting. Players shout not because they're angry. Quite the opposite, in fact, they shout because that's the only way you can get your orders across in the heat of the moment. The game operates at a wonderful intersection between chaos, competition (because you don't want to be responsible for the ship falling apart) and collaboration – because you absolutely have to work together... as a Spaceteam!

Spaceteam has been downloaded more than 4 million times, has won countless awards and has been almost universally lauded by reviewers, players and other game designers. It's simple and complex at the same time. It presents a level playing field for

experienced and new players and offers seasoned videogamers no advantage. Decades of experience with Street Fighter, Call of Duty or Halo aren't going to help you 'Eject the O-outlet'. Perhaps more than anything, though, Spaceteam is just plain good fun. Good, silly, fun.

But Spaceteam is also incredibly serious. Behind the absurdity of the 'Dangling Shunter', there is a careful, thoughtful, political project. Having quit his job at BioWare, Spaceteam creator Henry Smith is now firmly located in the world of independent game development and has a mission to make games in new ways and with new purposes.

The Spaceteam Admiral's Club is a way of supporting this work. It's inspired by the crowdfunding model of Kickstarter and there are exclusive rewards for joining. However, it differs from Kickstarter and its ilk in that it is not about financing the production of one specific title. By joining the Spaceteam Admiral's Club, you commit to supporting Henry's ongoing design work and enable the production of new, accessible games, for free, for everyone.

▶ Right: Spaceteam Admiral's Club medal (front and rear).

Steel Battalion Controller

2002

There is an adage in the world of Human Computer Interaction design that says that the ideal interface is transparent. Not literally transparent, although there are some neat PlayStation controllers with clear plastic cases. Transparency here means that the interface disappears, that it's intuitive, easy to understand and easy to use. It just gets out of the way and lets the user concentrate on what they're doing.

Think about a computer mouse. Once you get used to not picking it up to make the pointer move up the screen – and not shouting into it like it's a voice-control microphone – it's all pretty straightforward. It just gets out of the way and you get on with whatever you're doing. The same thing goes for touch-screens. Want to drag an object from one place to another? Drag it from one place to another, then. It's transparent. OK, the glass on a touch-screen is also transparent, but you get the point.

This notion applies to videogame interfaces. There's a school of thought that says they should get out of the way. If you have to think about the controls, then they're not transparent enough. If you have to think about which button to press to jump or fire, you'll get dragged out of the game because you'll be reminded you're just pressing buttons.

There's also a school of thought that says you should build an absolutely gigantic controller that has two massive joysticks, a throttle, and more than 40 buttons, including one for eject, which is under the kind of flip-up guard that you might expect to find on a fighter jet. There is even a set of pedals. This alternative school of thought on interaction design says that if players find the interface lacks transparency, they should stop complaining and practise some more.

Guess which school of thought Capcom's Production Studio 4 subscribes to?

Just in case you're still in any doubt, consider that, before you can even start controlling your Vertical Tank – the heavily armoured mechanical suit you pilot in the game – you have to start it up. This action alone takes multiple button presses that have to be precisely performed in a specific sequence.

Not many of these controllers were produced, making this a real collector's item, especially the first edition with green rather than blue buttons. However, at more than $200 each, you might not be able to collect that many – let alone lift them.

PLATFORM: MICROSOFT XBOX
DEVELOPER: CAPCOM PRODUCTION STUDIO 4
NUMBER OF BUTTONS: 40
CONTROL STICKS: 2
PEDALS: 3
DIFFERENCE BETWEEN FIRST AND SECOND EDITION CONTROLLERS: FIRST EDITION HAS GREEN BUTTONS, SECOND EDITION HAS BLUE

▲ Above: Game retail packaging.

▶ Right: First edition Steel Battalion controller (main) and details of second edition controls.

TOGGLE SWITCHES

VT-LOCATION MEA

OXYGEN SUPPLY
SYSTEM

BUFFER MATERIAL

FLT CONTROL
SYSTEM

FUEL FLOW RATE

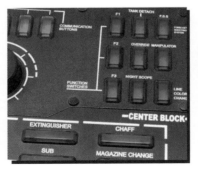

COMMUNICATION
BUTTONS

F1   TANK DETACH   F.S.S

F2   OVERRIDE MANIPULATOR

FUNCTION
SWITCHES

F3   NIGHT SCOPE

LINE
COLOR
CHANGE

CENTER BLOCK

EXTINGUISHER   CHAFF

SUB   MAGAZINE CHANGE

EJECT - CMD
WARNING
USE ONLY IN
EMERGENCY

LEVER
BUTTON
TRIGGER
N

OCKPIT HATCH
/ CLOSE

087.

Street Fighter II Animated Movie VHS cassette

1994

INFO

DIRECTED: GISABURO SUGII
SCREENPLAY: KENICHI IMAI
RUNNING TIME: 102 MINUTES
FEI LONG VOICED BY: MASAKATSU FUNAKI
(JAPAN), BRYAN CRANSTON (ENGLISH DUB)
US RATING: PG-13
UK RATING: 15

Street Fighter II: The Animated Movie is an anime adaptation of the Capcom's hugely popular and influential fighting game. Written by Kenichi Imai, the film documents the back-stories of characters including Chun-Li, Ryu and Sagat, and helps to further explain their rivalries, relationships and conflicts. The movie opens with a sequence in which Ryu delivers a devastating Shoryuken, scarring Sagat and setting up a feud that would continue not only through the film but throughout the Street Fighter videogame series.

There have actually been a surprisingly large number of different versions of the film since its original Japanese release in 1994. Two US versions exist, one of which is uncut from the original and one, rated PG-13, which makes edits to some of the bad language and, most notably, to a shower scene involving Chun-Li. This UK VHS release, released under license from Capcom by Manga UK, reinstates some of the profanity but similarly cuts the shower scene which remains far less revealing than in its original Japanese incarnation. This UK VHS release was given a 15 certificate by the British Board of Film Classification.

For owners of the PlayStation 2 and Xbox Street Fighter II Anniversary Collection, another cut of the film is

available as a bonus in the game's Gallery with a yet further edited version, available on Blu-Ray as part of the 2012 Street Fighter Anniversary Collector's Box. Adding in the Laser Disc, enhanced Blu-Ray/surround sound versions and the streaming version available via Netflix until 2012, the film has had almost as many different versions as the game on which its story is based!

On this VHS version, make sure you keep watching after the credits have finished rolling for a sneak preview of the *Street Fighter II* live action movie starring Kylie Minogue, Jean-Claude Van Damme and Raul Julia.

And of course, to complete the circle and make things even more confusing, shortly after the release of the animated movie, Capcom released Street Fighter II: Movie for the PlayStation and Sega Saturn. This game bore little in common with previous Street Fighter II instalments, being more of an interactive movie than a one-on-one fighting game. It also shouldn't be confused with the Street Fighter II: The Movie arcade game, which was based on the live action film and uses digitized graphics resembling those of Mortal Kombat. You are keeping up, right?

The influence of Street Fighter II: The Animated Movie can be seen on

the graphical style of the Street Fighter Zero (also known as Street Fighter Alpha) series which more closely resembles anime. Similarly, elements of the Animated Movie's storyline are adapted for inclusion in the game series' narrative.

If you managed to keep up with all the different edits and versions (and remember, we didn't even begin to talk about Widescreen editions, language dubs or subtitles), please reward yourself with a loud and well-earned You Win!

▲ Above: Stills from *Street Fighter II Animated Movie.*

▶ Right: *Street Fighter II Animated Movie* VHS packaging (PAL version).

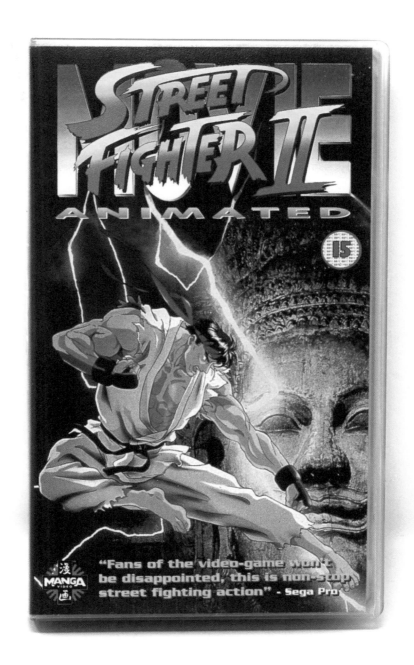

STREET FIGHTER II
ANIMATED

15

"Fans of the video-game won't
be disappointed, this is non-stop
street fighting action" - Sega Pro

MANGA
VIDEO

Super Bread Box

2013

#INFO

ORIGINAL SUPER CRATE BOX DESIGN AND CONCEPT: RAMI ISMAIL AND JAN WILLEM NIJMAN (VLAMBEER)

CONVERTED TO SUPER BREAD BOX FOR THE C64 BY: PAUL KOLLER

C64 SID MUSIC: MIKKEL HASTRUP INITIALLY DEVELOPED BY PAUL KOLLER FOR THE RGCD'S (RETRO GAMER CD) "C64 16KB CARTRIDGE GAME DEVELOPMENT COMPETITION" (IT WON)

AVAILABLE AS A DOWNLOAD AND DELUXE C64 CARTRIDGE EDITION ($30)

The past is the future. Ever since publishers and platform holders noticed that retro gaming really is commercially lucrative, they've mobilized different ways to reanimate their back catalogue. As the games industry is generally designed to eat itself every few years – the best game is always the next game... – the fact that they've managed to really explore retro is no small feat.

Nintendo now celebrate the playing of their past with the Virtual Console emulator on their modern machines. SEGA are plundering their back catalogue with mobile ports of their classics. There really has been no better time to explore the decades past of gaming. But what about the people who want to play modern games, but within the constraints of old, obsolete hardware?

Don't worry, demakes are for you.

The practice of remaking (demaking) games created for powerful, contemporary machines and attempting to fit them onto the impossibly small and underpowered hardware of the past is a fascinating area. Some amazing developers are performing feats of economy, focus and compression as they distil modern games into code that are mere fractions of their original size.

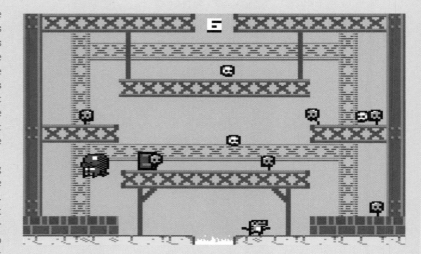

Super Crate Box was released by Vlambeer in 2010 for the PC. Developer Paul Koller, as part of the RGDC community 2012 development competition, attempted to make a version of it for the Commodore 64. Having won the competition, Paul went on to develop it into a full version, which was finally released on a Commodore 64 cartridge with full packaging.

Super Bread Box is a fantastic example of the demake discipline – and discipline it truly is. In analysing, distilling and focussing down games, the process of demaking reveals a uniquely personal take on what was important about the original. All extraneous elements are boiled away (and occasionally some non-extraneous ones too...) leaving only the absolute essence of the game behind. Demakes are a fascinating place to discover games at their purest.

▲ Above: Game-play screenshot.

▶ Right: Super Bread Box Commodore 64 cartridge and retail packaging.

Super FX Chip

1993

+INFO

DESIGNED BY: ARGONAUT GAMES
CODENAME: MARIO (MATHEMATICAL ARGONAUT ROTATION AND INPUT/OUTPUT)
GAMES INCLUDING THE SUPER FX CHIP: STAR FOX (KNOWN AS STARWING IN EUROPE), STUNT RACE FX (KNOWN AS WILD TRAX IN JAPAN), VORTEX, DIRT RACER, DIRT TRAX FX
STAR FOX 2 WAS DEVELOPED BUT NOT RELEASED FOR THE SNES. IT WAS RELEASED ON THE SNES CLASSIC EDITION IN 2017.
GAMES INCLUDING THE SUPER FX 2 CHIP: DOOM, SUPER MARIO WORLD 2 YOSHI'S ISLAND, WINTER GOLD

When the Super Nintendo Entertainment System launched at the beginning of the 1990s, one of the things that was immediately striking was its Mode 7 graphics. Amongst other things, Mode 7 allows programmers to take a background plane and tilt it to create the impression of perspective. Games such as Pilotwings and Super Mario Kart use this feature of Mode 7 to create the 3D effect of the ground and race tracks.

For gamers more used to 2D platform and shooting games, having this kind of 3D in the home was pretty much unheard of. Except that these weren't true 3D graphics. Look again at Super Mario Kart and you see that although the track (made up of that tilted background) can be moved around relatively smoothly, all the scenery objects and other karts rotate and scale in a much more jerky fashion. That's because they're still sprites – the separately drawn characters and objects that comprise everything that isn't the background.

So, just as with a traditional 2D platform game like Super Mario World, where every frame of Mario's animation is separately drawn, in a Mode 7 '3D' game like Super Mario Kart, each frame of a kart's rotation and each size that represents its distance from the viewer has to be drawn separately. Because Mode 7 only scales and manipulates the background, and because there are only a limited number of sprites that can be stored in memory, the inevitable result is a slight jerkiness as different sprites are swapped in and out.

While Mode 7 was undeniably impressive, the game designers at Nintendo were still frustrated that the system couldn't implement full 3D with karts and planes made from polygon models that could be freely rotated and scaled. So, that's why they developed a 3D graphics co-processor and called it the Super FX chip? Not exactly. They didn't. A UK developer called Argonaut did.

Developed under the code name 'MARIO' (Mathematical Argonaut Rotation And Input Ouput') and even having the acronym printed on the exterior of the final chip, Super FX was a custom-designed chip that gave the SNES the capability to render 3D polygons. The space shooting game Star Fox (renamed Starwing in Europe) was developed in part to showcase the enhanced graphics processing power. And showcase it, it most certainly did, bringing unprecedented 3D graphics to a home console.

Over time, the Super FX chip was further refined, with a version 2 model making its way into Super Mario World 2: Yoshi's Island, where it did slightly different duties. These focused more on complex sprite rotation and manipulating the game's giant end-of-level Boss creatures. It's worth remembering that, unlike console add-ons, adapters, and enhancers – such as Sega's 32X that added 3D rendering capabilities to the Mega Drive – the Super FX chip was actually built into each and every Star Fox cartridge.

Although it is the most famous such chip, and was prominently branded on Star Fox, the Super FX wasn't the only additional cartridge-based chip released for the SNES. Other chips added real-time clocks as well as advanced mathematical performance. In fact, this wasn't the first time Nintendo had added processors to their cartridge-based games. The Famicom had the ability to handle in-cart chips, such as those developed by Konami to provide additional sound capabilities. The non-Japanese NES didn't have this ability however, which explains why the Japanese music to Castlevania III sounds different to the US and European versions.

Next time you take apart a Nintendo cartridge, you might find more than you expected.

▲ Above: Starwing cartridge (PAL version) and internal circuit board with 'MARIO CHIP' marking.

Super Mario Sunshine:
Prima's Official Strategy Guide

2002

#INFO

WRITTEN BY: DAVID S. J. HODGSON, BRYAN STRATTON, STEPHEN STRATTON

PUBLISHED BY PRIMA GAMES IN 2002

RETAIL PRICE: $14.99, £12.99

SUPER MARIO SUNSHINE POSTCARDS INCLUDED: 4

NUMBER OF BLUE COIN LOCATIONS REVEALED: 240

1-UP MUSHROOM LOCATIONS REVEALED: 53

On one level, Strategy Guides – or walkthroughs as they are often known – seem pretty straightforward affairs. You play a game. You get stuck. You reach for the solution. Aha! So, that's how it's done. And before you know it, you're back on your way. Simple. Strategy Guides are for players who get stuck. So, they're for people who aren't very good at games? Or, worse still, they're for cheaters who give up too easily?

But maybe there's more to Strategy Guides. Consider this question. What is the point of videogames? We don't mean is playing them a waste of time. What we mean is what is the objective of a videogame? Is it to get the highest score? Is it to get to the end as quickly as possible? And what is the end? There's so many hidden items to find and hidden rooms to explore, so many secret characters to talk to and special missions to embark on. How could you possibly know if you had finished a game anyway? What if there was game-play lurking in there that you hadn't found? You've paid for that game-play! So, what does it mean to play a videogame? Well, that depends on what you want as a player.

If you want to find everything a game has to offer, you could do a lot worse than buy an Official Strategy Guide. Sure, this will help you on your way if you get stuck, but it will also help you locate all those ingeniously hidden items. Take Prima's Super Mario Sunshine guide as an example. If you want to race through the game, there's a 'Complete Quick-Path Walkthrough'. That's a no-nonsense, get me from the start to the end credits as quickly as you can route. But, for those wanting a more scenic tour, there's also an 'In-Depth Walkthrough Featuring Maps For Every Area'. There are 'Effective Solutions for All Minigames' and 'Comprehensive Boss Battle Techniques'. And, for the completist, the Guide proudly boasts that it reveals All Shine Sprites and exposes All Blue Coins!

And if you really worry that you might not have seen everything, there's even a 10-page Checklist that lets you literally tick off each Shine Sprite, Coin, 1-Up Mushroom, Nozzle Box and Yoshi Egg as you collect them. So, be in no doubt, once you've ticked every box, you've finished Super Mario Sunshine, and it's time to spend some money on the next game!

So, how are these glossy books different from the text-only walkthroughs and FAQs you find online? Is it just the fancy pictures and shiny paper? Not exactly. What makes these 'Official' guides is that they are

created with the assistance of the development teams and written alongside the game as it is developed. This means the writers of the guide have the inside knowledge of how the game works. It also means that they write solutions based on how the game is *supposed* to work and *supposed* to be played. That means you won't find any glitches that let you walk through walls, because who's going to admit their game doesn't work? If you want those sorts of glitchy game-play opportunities, that's when you go to an unofficial, fan-produced walkthrough.

▲ Above: Super Mario Sunshine Strategy Guide internal detail.

▶ Right: Super Mario Sunshine Strategy Guide cover.

Super Potato T-Shirt

• INFO

STORE MOTTO: 'GET YOUR WONDER SOFT WORLD'
T-SHIRT MAKER: TOMS CO LTD, TOKYO
SUPER POTATO AKIHABARA STORE ADDRESS:
101-0021 KITABAYASHI 3F/4F/5F BUILDING 1-11-2
SOTO-KANDA, CHIYODA-KU, TOKYO
T-SHIRT CARE INSTRUCTIONS: MACHINE WASH
WARM GENTLE, DO NOT USE CHLORINE BLEACH,
IRON AT MEDIUM SETTING, DO NOT DRY CLEAN

Can a videogame store be 'legendary'? Well, according to *Wired* magazine it can. What would it have to be to earn such an accolade? It should almost certainly be stacked almost to the point of overflowing with retro consoles, computers and controllers. It should definitely have more gaming merchandise than you've ever seen under one roof. Oh, and it should sell games. Lots and lots of games, for every conceivable system you've ever heard of, and ones that you haven't. In fact, it should be less like a shop and more like a museum. It should even have a place upstairs where you can get snacks and play arcade games while you ponder which games, plush toys and key rings you're going to purchase next when you go back down. All good so far.

Now, if it's going to be legendary, it's going to need a really cool name. Really cool. Something like Retro Game Paradise? Hmmm, not quite. OK, how about Joystick Junction. No, that's worse. Right, this is a bit out of leftfield but stay with me on this... how do you feel about calling it 'Super Potato'?

Perfect. And the mascot will be a little potato, right? And the potato will be super? You got it.

The main Super Potato store is located in the heart of Tokyo's Akihabara district. Known as 'Electric City', Akihabara is full of electronics stores selling anything from a single video cable to 80" flat screen TVs, and multi-storey arcades known as Game Centres that dedicate each of their many floors to different genres of games. These towers of play emblazoned with the logos of Sega and Taito are the most obvious places where it takes place, but videogaming is all around in Akihabara. Huge department stores like Yodobashi Camera and Sofmap have extensive ranges of videogames with vast numbers of PlayStation, PS Vita, Switch and 3DS titles along with guides and accessories, while in the Trader stores you'll also find limited editions and game soundtracks.

Super Potato is not the only game store in Akihabara. But it is different. For a start, it really does feel like a museum, with cases of collectible figures, plush toys of what seem to be quite marginal characters from game series (such as Tingle from The Legend of Zelda), early 1980s handheld games, and rows upon rows of carefully catalogued cartridges and discs.

And then there are consoles. Shelves of Famicom Disk Systems sit apparently just as happy being looked at as being purchased. There are Dreamcasts, PC Engines, Saturns... Each one has a unique price label that reflects the exact condition of the unit, taking into account any wear and tear or discolouration of the plastics.

But visiting Super Potato also feels like visiting an archive, or having a behind-the-scenes peek at a gallery's collections. Boxes of advertising flyers for console and arcade games are each presented in acid-free wallets and individually graded according to condition, taking into account any damage to corners or folds in the paper.

Of course, for many gamers, especially tourists visiting Akihabara, visiting Super Potato is almost an end in itself. What is surprising though, given its notoriety in game collecting circles, is how unassuming the store is. There is no grand entrance. Instead, you get a somewhat unwelcoming back alley that leads to some stairs, or an altogether-too-small lift that really reveals nothing of what awaits.

And like any tourist trip, you can't just go there, you have to buy the T-shirt too!

▶ Right: Super Potato T-shirt with store logo.

Taiko Drum Controller
2013

INFO

INTEGRATED STAND: YES
SOME ASSEMBLY REQUIRED: YES
NUMBER OF STICKS: 2
CONNECTION: VIA WII REMOTE
DRUM CAN BE HIT ON: HEAD OR RIM

Ever since the dawn of videogames, there have been some pretty unusual controllers. There have been countless joysticks with turbo buttons that can be used to fire off lasers and missiles faster than any human ever could. There are joysticks for fighting games that use military grade switches. Power Gloves, Robots, steering wheels, golf clubs, light guns... You name it and there's probably a videogame controller shaped like it. Sega even produced a fishing rod accessory for their Sega Bass Fishing game (which was also, and excellently, known as Get Bass). And over the years, there have been a number of musical controllers. The ones here are drums, but not just any drums. These aren't your average rock and roll drums that you might find on stage at Wembley or in Shea Stadium (or in your front room if you own a copy of Rock Band). No, these are ancient drums. Well, they're modelled after ancient drums. These are Taiko drums.

Taiko are Japanese drums with a history that dates back to the 6th century. Not the sixth generation of videogame console, but the sixth century. These things are old. But the Taiko we have here are designed for the Nintendo Wii and are just a little

more modern. This set was released in the 21st century, and is designed for use with the game Taiko no Tatsujin, which is usually translated into English as 'Taiko Master'.

Developed by Namco, Taiko no Tatsujin is a rhythm action game in which the player beats along to a number of backing tracks. But in case you think that sounds straightforward, it's not just a question of banging the drum with your sticks (not that that is easy to do when the songs get really tough). Just like real Taiko, there are different effects to be extracted by hitting the drum in different ways. So, you have single strikes and rolls, but also you have to distinguish between

hitting both the drum's skin and the rim around the edge.

The game was originally designed for the arcade and released in early 2001, with new versions still being developed today. In the arcade, the Taiko are big. Like really big. Which stands to reason, because arcades are big and because Taiko drums are really big. For the home console versions, the drums are dramatically scaled-down but there's no denying that the fun remains, especially in two player mode. Taiko Maestro, drum roll please...

▶ Right: Taiko Drum Japanese Wii U packaging and Wii controller.

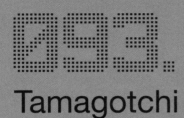

093.

Tamagotchi

1996

◆INFO

POWER: 2 X CR2032 BATTERIES
RELEASED: 1996 (JAPAN), 1997 (WORLDWIDE)
STAGES OF DEVELOPMENT FOR FIRST GENERATION
TAMAGOTCHI: 4
'SECRET' FIRST GENERATION TAMAGOTCHI CHARACTER:
BILL
BUTTONS: 3 (A=SELECT; B=EXECUTE (OR SWITCH TO
TIMER MODE); C=CANCEL)

On the face of it, the Tamagotchi is a pretty simple affair. According to creator Bandai, the name comes from combining the Japanese word 'tamag', which means 'egg', and the English word 'watch'. So, let's see how that works. An egg-shaped plastic case with a keychain houses a small LCD which displays the image of an egg. Once the unit's date and time are set, the on-screen egg eventually hatches to reveal a tiny virtual pet. Simple. Egg and Watch. That all makes sense so far.

Simple it might be, but it makes up for it by being incredibly demanding. The pet needs to be fed meals and snacks (it's a pretty simple diet of bread and candy). It needs to be played with (evidently virtual pets like simple guessing games). It even needs to be cleaned up (well, all that candy simply has to go somewhere). And, let's not forget that all of this happens on the pet's terms. It may not be convenient for you to clean them up right now but unless you do, they'll become sick. Is that what you want? Of course, you can toilet-train them if you are patient enough, which does make things a lot simpler for the owner.

Of course, the simplicity of the game-play is one thing, but it's the graphics and sound that are really notable for their economy. If you've seen more recent virtual pet games like Sony's EyeToy Pet for the PlayStation or Frontier Development's Kinectimals for Xbox and iOS, you'll be familiar with their ultra-realistic visuals, lovingly crafted animations and highly detailed sounds. Tamagotchi has none of these. The original Tamagotchi had a low resolution, black and white display that would make Minecraft look like a technology demo for a next generation graphics card, and sound for which the phrase 'some bleeps' is almost too generous. Even more recent incarnations of the Tamagotchi hardly deviate from the simple, almost simplistic, audiovisual blueprint set out in the mid-1990s.

And yet, for all the blocky graphics, for all the annoying bleeping in the middle of the night, each Tamagotchi is undeniably cute. And players get attached to them. Really attached to them. To the point where they feel a genuine emotional connection with them; a genuine sadness and sense of loss if their Tamagotchi should pass away. The Tamagotchi effect is so strong that the phrase is used by psychologists to describe the feeling of emotional attachment that people sometimes feel for otherwise inanimate objects. It's surprising to think how few frames of animation and how few bleeps and squeaks it takes a skilled animator and sound designer to create a believable character that players invest time, money and emotions into.

On the subject of what happens to Tamagotchis when they get sick or old, it all depends on where you are in the world. In many Japanese versions, Tamagotchi do indeed pass away. However, in Europe the situation is a bit different. According to *The Official Tamagotchi Pet Care Guide And Record Book*, published in the UK in 1997, 'All Tamagotchis have come to this planet to be with wonderful Earth parents for a while. But, they all eventually fly back to their home planet because they get very homesick for it.'

And the name of the Tamagotchi home planet? Well that will be Tamagotch of course. Simple.

◀ Right (top): Tamagotchi and original packaging.

▶ Right (bottom): The Official Tamagotchi Pet Care Guide and Record Book (UK).

094

Team
Mystic Pendant

2016

#INFO

POKÉMON PIKACHU'S 4 MOODS: 1. HATES YOU; 2. IS OK WITH YOU; 3. LIKES YOU; 4. LOVES YOU
STEPS NEEDED TO EARN 1 WATT: 20
TEAM MYSTIC PENDANT DIMENSIONS: 55MM X 49MM
CHAIN LENGTH: 282MM

It's fair to say that Pokémon Go has been something of a success. Since it was released in July 2016, the free-to-play Augmented Reality game has been breaking records left, right and centre. *The Guinness Book of World Records* recognized it as grossing more revenue than any other mobile phone game in its first month, and within just a couple of months, it had made over $500 million and had been downloaded more than half a billion times.

The prospect of catching Pokémon in the real world is clearly a compelling one. Niantic, the game's developer, had originally come to life as a start-up company within Google. They created a perfect storm of mobile technology, GPS, map data and a seemingly inexhaustible supply of little (and not so little) monsters.

But where other Pokémon games invite you to role play as a trainer and transport you to a magical, far-away land, Pokémon Go reveals that the rare and legendary beasts were around us all the time. In the centre of town. At school. In the office car park. And gone is the role playing. In Pokémon Go, you are a trainer and, though your phone lets you fire off Pokéballs and shows you the locations of nearby wildlife, if you want to catch em all, you need to get walking.

Once you've started collecting, and amassed a good stock of berries, potions and eggs to go with your Pokémon, the nice, gentle part of the game takes a back seat as the battling begins. Once you're beyond Level 5, you can finally head to a Gym and take the fight to the other local trainers.

But before you do, there is an important choice to make. No, not which Pokémon to enter into the Gym, though this is significant for sure. The really important choice to make is which Team to join. There are three choices, each with their own colour, leader and Pokémon mascot.

Team Instinct (yellow) is led by Spark, and has Zapdos as its mascot. Team Valor (red) is headed up by Candela, accompanied by Moltres. Team Mystic (blue) is fronted by Blanche, with Articuno as its standard-bearer.

Which should you choose? It's up to you, but choose carefully, as there are real rivalries between teams and your allegiance is one of the key means of identifying yourself within the vast global community of players. The pendant in the picture belongs to a Team Mystic player. You don't have to wear it to play the game. But it couldn't hurt.

Although it is far and away the most famous example, Pokémon Go isn't the first time the little critters have got players up on their feet and racing around. In the late 1990s, Nintendo released Pokémon Pikachu, a virtual pet and pedometer which required the player to care for their electric mouse friend by walking. The more steps taken, the more Pikachu's friendship levels increase.

▲ Above: Pokémon Pikachu portable system and pedometer.

▶ Right: Team Mystic pendant and chain with Pokémon Go running on iOS.

095.
Temporary Tattoos
2017

●INFO

MOSHI MONSTERS RELEASED: 16 APRIL 2008
REGISTERED MOSHI MONSTERS USERS IN 2018:
OVER 100 MILLION
ANGRY BIRDS STAR WARS RELEASED: 8 NOVEMBER 2012
DOWNLOADS OF ANGRY BIRDS STAR WARS IN 2013
(ALL PLATFORMS): OVER 100 MILLION
A 2012 HARRIS POLL SUGGESTED THAT 1 IN 5 US
ADULTS HAS AT LEAST ONE TATTOO

You've got shelves full of limited-edition box sets of the games you've pre-ordered. You have every console old and new, from the Magnavox to the Xbox One X. You have countless T-shirts with videogame designs ranging from the easily recognizable Space Invaders to the altogether more esoteric collection of Splatoon ink splats. You have PlayStation cufflinks and a Namco hat. It's fair to say that you are a gamer. But all of these things are fleeting and ephemeral. Those T-shirts will eventually fade in the wash or wear out altogether, there will inevitably be more games to pre-order and, let's face it, the Xbox One X is unlikely to be the last videogame console ever made.

What about a more lasting record of your love of games? Something that won't just fade away after a few years or become obsolete. Something that will be with you forever. Something that will be on you forever – a part of you. That's it! A gaming tattoo!

The only question now is what design to choose. Something simple like a Triforce? Or perhaps something even more obscure like ↑↑↓↓←→←→ B A?

That's the infamous 'Konami Code' that unlocked cheat modes in so many classic videogames of the 1980s and 90s. Or there's the iconic geometric PlayStation symbols, the Portal logo, or the Dreamcast swirl... There are just so many options.

Choices, choices. Perhaps you're not quite ready for the ultimate, lifetime commitment of a tattoo. You really like Moshi Monsters now but can you be 100 per cent certain that you're still going to want Sweet Tooth the Candy Criminal and C.L.O.N.C. agent on your arm when you're in your retirement? And maybe Angry Birds Star Wars is a game you play a lot at the moment, but can you be absolutely sure an Imperial Pigtrooper logo is what you want to be rolling up your sleeve and talking about with your children and grandchildren in decades to come?

It's perfectly possible that it is. There's no doubting that Moshi Monsters and Angry Birds are great games. But just in case you're in any doubt about inking yourself in perpetuity, there is a safer option. Treat yourself to a temporary tattoo. You get to literally wear the object of your fandom on your sleeve, and if you change your mind, a long soak in the bath is all you need to reset things. Or think of it this way: before you make that commitment permanent, you can try out some designs for a while. Until the next time you take a shower, at least.

▲ Above: Tattoos before application.

▶ Right: Angry Birds Star Wars and Moshi Monsters temporary tattoos.

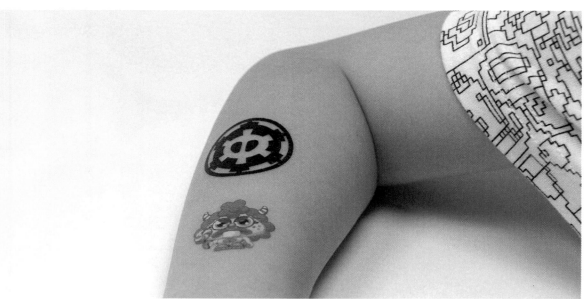

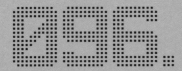

096.
Tingle
Plush Toy
2013

◆INFO

TINGLE CHARACTER CREATED BY: TAKAYA IMAMURA
FIRST APPEARANCE: THE LEGEND OF ZELDA: MAJORA'S MASK
CATCHPHRASE: 'TINGLE! TINGLE! KOOLOO-LIMPAH!'
SIBLINGS: ANKLE, KNUCKLE AND DAVID JR.
TINGLE TOY PURCHASED IN: SUPER POTATO, AKIHABARA, TOKYO
MADE IN: CHINA

The cuddly toy. If you want to know that you've made it as a cultural icon, you just need to ask yourself one thing. Is there a cuddly toy of me? If the answer is yes, you're up there with Super Mario, Pac-Man and Pikachu. That's certainly illustrious company right there. Internationally recognized, global icons. You're on the A-List without a doubt. If the answer is no, there's absolutely no reason to be disheartened. It takes time. You just have some work to do building up your visibility and brand recognition. Rome wasn't built in a day. Do you think that superstars like Sonic the Hedgehog, the Sheep from Minecraft or Tingle just broke into the big time overnight?

Hold on a minute, The Sheep from Minecraft has a plush toy? Well, I guess sheep are pretty fluffy and cuddly. And there aren't a huge number of lovable creatures in Minecraft. You wouldn't want to go to bed clutching a Creeper for comfort would you? (What's that, there are Creeper cuddly toys?)

OK, Creepers, Sheep, Ocelots, you get the picture. Minecraft is a hugely popular game so that's fair enough. But, what's a Tingle? Is that another Minecraft Mob? Seriously? Tingle's from The Legend of Zelda?

According to Nintendo, and character designer Takaya Imamura,

Tingle is a 35-year-old obsessed with Forest Fairies who dresses in a green costume and has an uncanny resemblance to Link. Tingle first appeared in The Legend of Zelda: Majora's Mask and has subsequently played a role in The Wind Waker, Four Swords Adventures and The Minis Cap. Additionally, he makes cameos in The Phantom Hourglass, Spirit Tracks, Skyward Sword and the Hyrule Warriors Majora's Mask Downloadable Content Pack. His incomparable image is even available as an unlockable costume on Super Mario Maker.

Tingle even has his own spinoff game, the excellently and lengthily titled Freshly-Picked Tingle's Rosy Rupeeland for the Nintendo DS handheld. This was released in September 2006 in Japan and just over a year later in Europe.

You'll notice that Freshly-Picked Tingle's Rosy Rupeeland didn't get a US release. That seems strange. Well, according to current Legend of Zelda producer Eiji Aonuma, it was felt that Americans didn't warm to Tingle – in fact, one US review unkindly likened Tingle to Jar Jar Binks from The Phantom Menace! As such, not only was Tingle's game not released but, on top of that, the character wasn't included in The Twilight Princess either. Poor Tingle.

This, coupled with the complex back-story and eccentric appearances in Zelda games have ensured that Tingle has become something of a cult character among videogame fans. This plush toy was purchased in the Super Potato videogame store in Tokyo's Akihabara district. So, while Tingle might seem like a marginal character at first, there is more to this would-be Forest Fairy than meets the eye. Viewed in this light, Tingle is utterly deserving of cuddly toy status.

Or as Tingle would say, 'Tingle! Tingle! Kooloo-Limpah!'

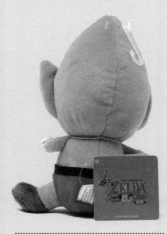

▲ Above: Tingle Plush Toy (rear), with 'Wind Waker HD' label.

▶ Right: Tingle Plush Toy (front).

Vice City map 1997

◉INFO

DIMENSIONS: 420MM X 295MM
NUMBER OF HOSPITALS: 3
MOST NORTHERLY POINT: MIRAMIRE
MOST EASTERLY POINT: VICE BEACH
MOST SOUTHERLY POINT: RICHMAN HEIGHTS
MOST WESTERLY POINT: LITTLE BOGOTA AND
LITTLE DOMINICA
SUGGESTED FOR: MATURE AUDIENCES

More than any other game – and possibly more than any other entertainment product in any other media form – Grand Theft Auto can be guaranteed to upset sections of the mainstream media. It's not the most wholesome accolade, but no-one could argue that Rockstar Games hasn't worked hard for it. It's a shame that the controversy often draws attention from the achievements. GTA truly is one of the most sophisticated, media-literate, detailed works ever created, and all without once resorting to common decency.

In its original release, Grand Theft Auto looked very different from the super-polished 3D world that people recognize today. The first iteration of what was to rapidly grow into one of the most commercially and critically successful franchises in history was much more modest.

DMA Design, creators of Lemmings, gave the world a top-down, graphically primitive action game that proved reasonably successful, but it laid the foundations for what was to follow. Much has been written about Grand Theft Auto being about freedom, building on some of the principles first established by the space-trading game 'Elite' back in the 80s, but GTA brings a different kind of playground. At the risk of over-simplifying, freedom in

outer-space is relatively easy to create. There's an infinite amount of space, and you are free to move within it. What GTA granted the player was the freedom to do what they liked within a dense, complicated environment that would usually fight back. On opening the cardboard box packaging of the original game in 1997, three items would spill out that supported that freedom and underlined the illusion of the game.

GTA takes place in three cities, and the player is provided with three maps to navigate them by. Of course, players have been given maps for games before, but these often tended towards the Tolkienesque in their brevity. A few key landmarks were typically drawn, with great swathes of barren land between them. These maps were different – these were dense, detailed and street-level correct.

To play the game with the maps laid out next to you is to allow the adventure to spill tangibly out into your home. With a friend sat beside you helping to navigate the complex streets as you track your quarry (or run from the cops), the illusion of truly inhabiting Liberty City is intoxicating. More than any sophisticated on-screen way-finding, having the physical map to hand gave

you a believable world to enjoy this unprecedented freedom in. The map was true, which in turn reinforced the world you were playing in. It didn't feel like a game had been designed around a map, it felt like the publishers had kindly made a map of the city into a game. Counter-intuitively, the freedom felt all the more complete because the boundaries were clear. The game didn't try to pretend otherwise. Maps have edges. Even GTA has city limits.

▲ Above: Vice City map details.

▶ Right: Map of Vice City (front and rear).

098.
Virtual Boy
1995

#INFO

DEVELOPMENT CODENAME: VR32
TECHNOLOGY LICENSED FROM: REFLECTION TECHNOLOGY
UNITS SOLD: 770,000
PROCESSOR: NEC V810
POWER: 6 X AA BATTERIES
CONTROLLER LAYOUT: 2 X D-PADS, A, B, START, SELECT
DISPLAYS: 1 PER EYE
AUTOMATIC PAUSE: EVERY 15-30 MINUTES
DISPLAY COLOUR: RED (VERY)

In the mid-1990s, Nintendo was riding high. Its NES/Famicom system had been a runaway success, the Game Boy was the bestselling handheld console by far, and the Super Nintendo Entertainment System was already looking set to confirm Nintendo's position as one of the leaders in videogaming.

Nonetheless, the company couldn't afford to be complacent, especially with competition looming in the form of Sony's PlayStation and Sega's Saturn. With its own next generation home console still in development (and known as Project Reality before being renamed the Nintendo 64), what Nintendo needed was something that would demonstrate its technological superiority. The answer, or so it thought, would come in the form of Virtual Reality. What could be more futuristic? Or wrong.

On the face of it, it should have been a perfect match. Cutting edge technology, a company that had helped redefine videogaming in the 1980s and 1990s, all headed up by chief engineer Gunpei Yokoi, whose previous success had included the Game & Watch and Game Boy. Unfortunately, a combination of issues meant that the Virtual Boy never really caught on. The

technology wasn't quite as impressive as had been hoped, and design compromises affected how the system looked, felt, and handled.

Released in Japan and the US in 1995, the system is an odd-looking one for sure. Although there had been discussions about head tracking systems and head mounted displays more like modern VR, Nintendo opted for a tabletop design. This lends the Virtual Boy the look of a pair of binoculars that have sprouted legs and are about to walk off. Indeed, some of the US TV advertising portrayed the console stalking around in just this manner.

If the lack of head tracking was one compromise, another was the decision to opt for monochrome rather than full-colour displays. If you thought the Virtual Boy looked red on the outside, wait till you look through the viewfinder. Everything is black and red. This may have made for a smoother experience given the power of the system, but it didn't exactly match up to the vision of the future that consumers were expecting.

And then there were the health warnings. Perhaps Nintendo was being overcautious, but the warning that the system wasn't suitable for children under seven years old may

not have helped sales. Although, given that many reviewers and players complained about headaches after using the Virtual Boy and the system itself paused every 15 minutes asking you if you were sure you wanted to continue, maybe Nintendo wasn't being overcautious after all.

It would be easy to say the Virtual Boy was a failure or that it was rushed to market in an unfinished state. In commercial terms, fewer than 800,000 units were sold, and the system was never released outside Japan or the US. As a result, only 22 games were ever produced for the system. However, it wasn't Nintendo's first attempt to get into stereoscopic 3D, nor would it be the last. The glasses-based Famicom 3D System released in Japan in 1987 had marked a first foray, while the 3DS finally proved successful in offering 3D after years of hints that Nintendo might add 3D features to the Nintendo 64 and GameCube consoles. As for VR, the company still hasn't formally committed, though it has been making some teasing suggestions about it in relation to the Switch for some time... But it seems as though, for a while yet, the Virtual Boy is the closest thing we have to Nintendo VR. Just remember to take a break every 15 minutes.

▲ Above: Nintendo Virtual Boy
tabletop console and controller.

Virtual Reality Headsets 2014-17

ACCESSORIES IN THE VIVE PRE BOX: 3-IN-1 CABLE (ATTACHED); AUDIO CABLE (ATTACHED); SHORT USB CABLE; POWER ADAPTERS (2); MICRO USB CABLES (2)

CLEANING CLOTH: INCLUDED

INSTRUCTIONS ON HOW TO CLEAN THE VIVE PRE FACE CUSHION: DAMPEN WITH A CLEAN CLOTH WITH COLD WATER, AIR DRY AT ROOM TEMPERATURE. DO NOT TUMBLE DRY OR EXPOSE TO DIRECT SUNLIGHT. DO NOT SCRUB OR BLEACH THE FACE CUSHION

GOOGLE CARDBOARD RELEASED: 25 JUNE 2014

UNITS SHIPPED: 10 MILLION

DEVELOPMENT KITS: CARDBOARD SDK (ANDROID, IOS, JAVA, UNITY)

Although thinkers like Myron Krueger had used terms such as 'Artificial Reality' to describe computing systems since the 1970s, the invention of the phrase 'Virtual Reality' is usually attributed to artist, scientist, visionary and former Atari employee, Jaron Lanier. Since coining the term in 1987, it has become almost a byword for the promise of computing. For a long time, the sense of 'being there', of immersion or presence in a simulated environment, was pretty much the province of science fiction or the multi-million dollar labs of organizations such as NASA.

Every so often, however, VR makes a break for the living room. Newspapers and magazines are full of headlines claiming that this year, or next year, is 'the year of virtual reality'. For many years, these claims have fallen flat when technologies haven't matched the hype. Head mounted displays have been bulky. Graphics have been plagued by latency and low resolution images and the actuality of virtuality has been a slightly nauseous combination of motion sickness and disappointment.

However, in the late 2010s, things seemed a little different. Fewer low resolutions and jittery images. Less bulky. Less headache and vomit-inducing. Could it be that this year, or maybe next year, really is the year of virtual reality? We've heard it before, certainly. But the technology has never been this good before.

To get a sense of how things are shaping up, here are some HMDs (Head Mounted Displays) along with the altogether more affordable Google Cardboard phone adapter.

Oculus Rift DK2

The DK2 (Development Kit 2) began shipping in 2014. It includes several updates on previous Oculus hardware including higher-resolution displays (960 x 1080 per eye) with higher refresh rates. In 2015, Oculus announced that over 100,000 DK2 units had been shipped.

HTC Vive Pre

The HTC Vive is a virtual reality headset developed by HTC and Valve Corporation. The Vive Pre is a near-complete version that was showcased at the Consumer Electronics Show in 2016. The Vive was initially compatible only with Windows-based computers. However, In June 2017, HTC and Valve announced that the Vive and SteamVR would be coming to the Apple Mac platform. Following a $200 price drop, the Vive costs approximately $600.

Google Cardboard

This is a low cost VR platform developed by Google and designed for use with a mobile phone running compatible applications. The phone fits into the back of the viewer itself, which is equipped with two lenses that create a stereoscopic 3D effect. As of the beginning of 2017, Google announced that over 10 million Cardboard viewers had been shipped and that over 1,000 applications were available. How low cost is low cost VR in 2017? The official Google headset costs around $15, but shop around and you can pick up them up for just a few pennies (though you'll need a compatible phone, which might cost a fraction more).

▶ Right: HTC Vive headset (top left), HTC Vive controller (top right), Google Cardboard (middle), Oculus Rift DK2 (bottom).

Samsung Gear VR

Released in 2015 and developed by Samsung and Oculus, the Gear VR is a mobile headset that uses a compatible Samsung Galaxy or Note phone as its display. Since the initial release, there have been a number of revisions of the headset which have added compatibility with the latest high end mobile phones such as the Note 8 in late 2017. Although the Gear VR was launched in 2015, Samsung had been researching the use of mobile phone based virtual reality for many years and had been awarded a patent in 2005. At that time, however, mobile displays were not of a high enough quality and processors were not speedy enough to deliver the low latency that Samsung required.

Playstation VR

Developed under the codename Project Morpheus and released in late 2016, PlayStation VR is a head mounted display designed to work with the PlayStation 4 console. The headset has a 5.7 inch OLED display and is capable of outputting video to a television. This feature allows spectators to see what the PlayStation VR headset wearer is experiencing and is referred to as a 'Social Screen'.

In late 2017, Sony offered a free 14-day in-home trial of PlayStation VR to PlayStation Plus subscribers. Unsurprisingly, the offer of a trial of the headset, PlayStation Camera, two Move controllers, a copy of Skyrim VR along with the option to purchase the set for a heavily discounted price after the trial period, meant the 1400 trials were snapped up in double quick time.

....

▲ Above: Samsung Gear VR headset.

▶ Right: PlayStation Move controller and PSVR Headset.

100.
wipEout:
The Music
1995

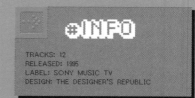

●INFO

TRACKS: 12
RELEASED: 1995
LABEL: SONY MUSIC TV
DESIGN: THE DESIGNER'S REPUBLIC

'Do not underestimate the Power of PlayStation' was the tagline for Sony's first foray into the world of videogame console manufacturing. You could be forgiven for thinking that this was just over-the-top marketing hyperbole but, on closer inspection, there is more to this than might have met the eye – or ear – in 1994.

The system's impact on graphics is well documented, with launch games like Namco's Ridge Racer bringing arcade-quality 3D into the home. Sure, there had been 3D games on console and PC before, but this was a system built from the ground up for 3D gaming. So, the PlayStation looked different. But it also sounded different.

Mega Drive and SNES games certainly had more complex and richer sound than the Master System and NES systems before them. And PC gamers were already used to adding high-end sound cards whose MIDI-controlled FM sounds were orders of magnitude more sophisticated than the simple bleeps of unexpanded systems. But these games definitely still sounded like games, and you couldn't mistake the sound of Donkey Kong Country on the SNES, Sonic the Hedgehog on the Mega Drive, or The Secret of Monkey Island 2's Bone Song for the music in the charts. Now, you might argue that that's a good thing, and plenty of

people to this day celebrate videogame music compositions and composers, but that's often precisely because the music does sound distinctive and different – like videogame music.

But with the PlayStation, all that changed. Ridge Racer had a manic European techno soundtrack blasting out that felt like it had been transplanted straight from a rave in a Rotterdam warehouse. But, for a really decisive illustration of the PlayStation's sonic credentials, wipEout was the top of the pops.

Developed by the legendary UK game studio Psygnosis, who were acquired by Sony just prior to the PlayStation's launch, wipEout was a futuristic racing game oozing with popular cultural references and almost achingly hip in its presentation. The artwork, logos and typography in the game – and even on the packaging itself – were created with the assistance of renowned design studio The Designer's Republic, whose work you might have seen on Warp or The Orb album covers. Even the capital 'E' in the wipEout logo seemed to be a reference to the notorious recreational drug that was filling newspaper column inches, and inspiring popular cultural anthems like The Shamen's 'Ebeneezer Goode'. By 1994, we'd come quite a long way from Pac-Man. If videogaming had been seen as

uncool in the early 1990s, Sony's PlayStation marketing turned things around. Consoles were installed in the chill-out rooms of UK superclubs like Cream and Ministry of Sound, so you could play wipEout with the tunes still banging away in your head.

And it wasn't just about putting games in clubs. It was about putting club music in games. With tracks by The Chemical Brothers, Leftfield, and Orbital, the soundtrack to wipEout was about as far from chiptunes as you could imagine. And these weren't re-imaginings of those tracks. These were the actual tracks – note for note, byte for byte.

Do not underestimate the power of the PlayStation's CD-ROM drive.

▲ Above: wipEout game-play screenshot.

▶ Right: wipEout soundtrack packaging and compact disc inlay.

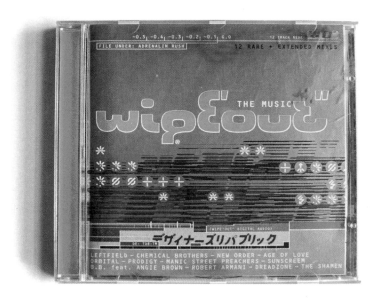

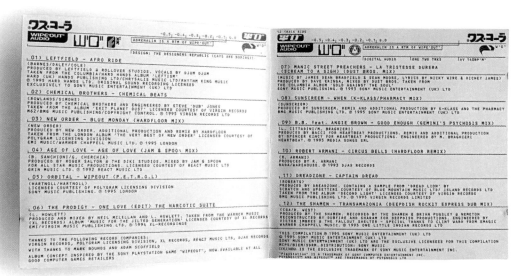

INDEX

CREDITS

Photography: Eve Bentley, Allen Coombs, James Newman,
Iain Simons

All images supplied by NVA with the exception of those sourced
from Alamy, Atari, Bethesda Softworks LLC, CAPCOM, Evan-
Amos, Gamershell.com, NAMCO, Nintendo, Psygnosis, Sinclair
Research, Sony Interactive Entertainment, Stone Oakvalley,
Ubisoft, Vlambeer, RGCD and Shutterstock.com.

WITH THANKS TO

Jonathan Smith, Karl Hilton, Alison Beasley, Ian Livingstone, Masayuki
Uemura, Carl Cavers, Andy Payne, Masaya Matsuura, Miles Jacobson,
Henry Smith, Jason Tomlin, iShadowCat, Keita Takahashi, Philip and
Andrew Oliver aka The Oliver Twins, Richard Jones, Eric Kale, and the
brilliant team at The National Videogame Arcade.
Lucy & Martha Newman.
Sarah & Tom Simons.

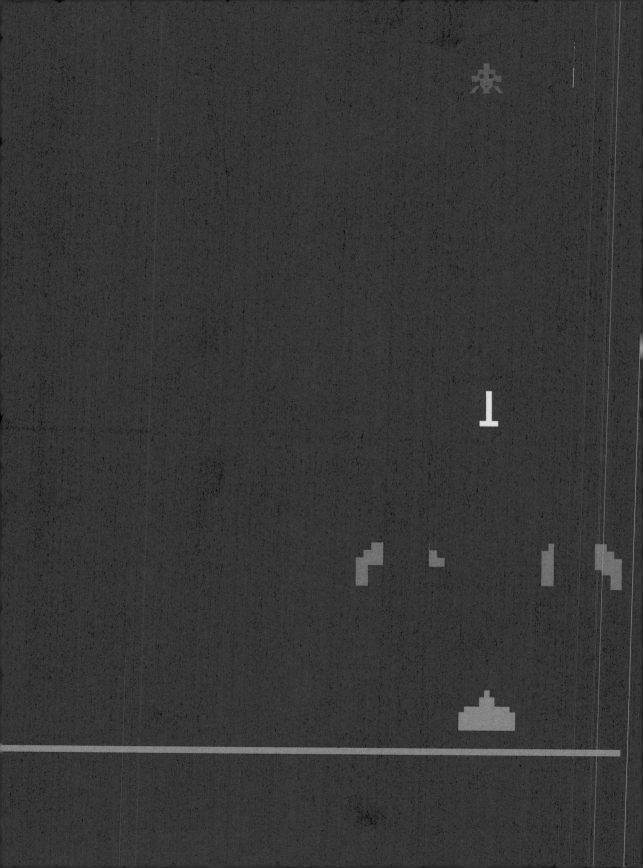